12.31.73

THE HUMAN FUTURES SERIES

Barry N. Schwartz and Robert L. Disch,
General Editors

Barry N. Schwartz, editor of this volume in the Human Futures series, is Assistant Professor of Communication Arts at New York City Community College, and Director of the Cultural Alternatives Network. He is the author of *Hard Rains, White Racism, Killing Time,* and *THE NEW HUMANISM: Art in a Time of Change,* and editor of *Affirmative Education* (Prentice-Hall, 1972).

human connection
and the new media

human connection and the new media

EDITED BY *Barry N. Schwartz*

PRENTICE-HALL, INC. *Englewood Cliffs, N.J.*

Library of Congress Cataloging in Publication Data

SCHWARTZ, BARRY N   comp.
   Human connection and the new media.

   (The Human futures series)   (A Spectrum Book)
      CONTENTS: Fuller, R. B. Utopia or oblivion.—Widmer, K. Sensibility
under technocracy: reflections on the culture of processed communications.—
Lilly, J. Mental health and communication.—[etc.]
   1. Communication—Social aspects—Addresses, essays, lectures. 2. Mass media—
Social aspects—Addresses, essays, lectures. 3. Social values—Addresses, essays,
lectures. I. Title. II. Series. [DNLM: 1. Communication. 2. Human engi-
neering.   HM258 S399h 1973]
HM258.S29   301.14   73–7740
ISBN 0–13–444752–2
ISBN 0–13–444745–X (pbk.)

We are grateful to the Laboratory for Planetary Studies and
the National Astronomy and Ionosphere Center of Cornell
University for permission to reprint in duplicate the dia-
gram of the engraved plate affixed to *Pioneer 10.*

10 9 8 7 6 5 4 3 2 1

PRENTICE-HALL INTERNATIONAL, INC. (*London*)
PRENTICE-HALL OF AUSTRALIA PTY. LTD. (*Sydney*)
PRENTICE-HALL OF CANADA LTD. (*Toronto*)
PRENTICE-HALL OF INDIA PRIVATE LIMITED (*New Delhi*)
PRENTICE-HALL OF JAPAN, INC. (*Tokyo*)

contents

*This book is dedicated to
Professor Herman Krinsky,
who gave so generously to me
in my time of need*

human connection
and the new media

introduction
humanism and the new media

The technological pattern dominant in our time has generally spawned imitative processes throughout all disciplines. Artists, historians, critics, social philosophers and others have adopted a pseudo-scientific posture in their work which, in the extreme, is expressed as a formalism divorced from human values. The school administrator, whose function is to expedite and assist the learning process, now substitutes administration, with its rules, regulations, and bureaucratic mechanisms for the very educational experience which was once, but is no longer, primary. The art critic no longer explicates creative works, but now insists that art is a demonstration of his formalist biases. Industries which once directed their efforts toward servicing the needs of people now spend much of their operating budgets trying to convince people of needs they don't know they have.

Research and learning in most disciplines and activities is motivated by "correct" methods and not by a search for value. A glance at recent Ph.D. thesis titles is all that is needed to demonstrate to what extent specialists are the technicians of the technological order. Human inquiry now rests secure in the belief that the ways in which we work are more important than the purposes to which our efforts are directed.

During the past year I completed work on a book about the new humanism.[1] The same year I worked intimately with three

[1] Readers may wish to consult *THE NEW HUMANISM: Art in a Time of Change* (New York: Praeger Publishers, 1974).

others who were pioneering one of the new media, videotape. As we went along, we attempted to discern the general qualities and specific grammar of this new and decidedly crucial tool for communication. In many ways this volume represents a synthesis of these two seemingly different interests. However, the integration of the communication media with the developing humanist value system is vital to our future, and their combination is necessary if the new media are to serve to free us from the oppressions of our time.

As well as possessing certain characteristics common to all communication media, the new media do have inherent qualities and distinct impacts. The spatial, temporal and feedback properties of these media are capable of diverse uses, some very positive, and some that are highly manipulative. The integration of a humanist value system with the new media leads to an ethics, a code of media conduct, an awareness of those uses of the new media specifically designed to manipulate, distort, confuse and control. A media ethics would further set guidelines for the use of another's information and do much to create a climate of opinion, one that might become law, curtailing the most insidious uses of media. Unless we extend Humanistic ethics into the electronic environment we will have the right to speak, but not to program; the right to assembly, but not to connection; the right to due process but no way to influence the judgments of computers.

Values that emanate from words and not acts are doomed to stagnation. As ethical propositions, academic verbiage, moral persuasions, and philosophic leanings, verbalized values do little more than provide new course content in obsolete curricula or bolster sales of books young people are forced to read. But if values without application are futile, new information without new values is equally useless. The truth alone will not set us free. The new media will only be of enduring promise if their potential contribution to the humanizing and liberating movements of our time is realized. Thus the new media will come to be used for new purposes only when the new media and new values are indivisible. The new media and the new information they generate will change little if the prevailing value system remains intact.

For all the talk of information overload, we seem to be in a situation better described as value overload. If we change our values, then our lives, we will find that we know too little, not too much. The existing value system, propped as it is on the commercial and exploitive drives to profit and control, nullifies the potential of all new developments. Marshall McLuhan not withstanding, new developments will be undermined if old values direct what we do with what we learn.

If social change is to accelerate at the same rate as technological change we need complete access to all information and to a communication system that is able to transmit both knowledge of events *and* our reaction to them. Unfortunately, in the world of the thinking, print still reigns supreme. Those who address themselves critically and creatively to the social patterns that affect them still do so after the fact. We have generated a situation in which the intelligentsia survives as a media-underprivileged group, while the average citizen, whose ability to read and utilize the print media itself is limited, remains a passive recipient of programmed learning.

Unlike print, which today maintains vast separations among people, the new media are holistic, which is to say that they bring together what societies and traditional media have kept apart. The new media have accurately been called the central nervous system of humanity, connecting human beings much the same way the individual's nervous system connects him to his body.

The new media, being holistic, tend to promote group processes and therefore lead us away from the fragmentations of unshakable individualism and collective mechanism. Their communal quality permits group processes within which there is enormous potential for individuality and unique expression. In some sense, the new media promote a vision of every man becoming the artist of his experience. This vision, of course, assumes that the tools will get into the hands of the people.

The existing mass media now promote passivity, and passivity deadens creativity. Many people, out of touch with their own creativity, expect technology to do what they have thus far failed to do for themselves. The new media are important—we cannot do without them—but they are not going to do something for us without us. If we are to get out of the contemporary crisis, we will need new tools; but new tools themselves will not get us out of our social, cultural and spiritual dilemma. If the new media are harnessed by the existing value system, they will only help us to continue to do what we already do, only now more effectively.

The new media I have chosen for discussion affect our communication in at least two ways. Some are able to extend man's ability to communicate. Others are able to enlarge man's capacity for communication. Some, like holography, make it possible to communicate information that would have previously been inaccessible. Some, like videotape, make it possible to inform large numbers of people through intense learning experiences. Biofeedback, on the other hand, enables a person to communicate with his body in ways that give the mind and body more information about each other. To the general reader, ESP, telepathy, and even interstellar communication phenomena may seem removed from his communication experiences, but to dismiss them for this reason is foolish. Today they are viable communication media employed by growing numbers of people. To call a conception of communication potential "science fiction" is to pay it a compliment. Science fiction today usually deals with a probable future.

The new media *do have* enormous potential for democratizing the decision-making apparatuses of society. They are capable of instantly dispelling misconceptions which otherwise would mold our history. They are capable of leaving nothing to the imaginative powers of fear, distrust, and false conception. They render reality in greater focus and contribute to human understanding. They are communication media, and, as John Lilly suggests later in this book, the ability to communicate has a direct relationship to mental health, well-being, and humanness. Thus, while the world polarizes itself into noxious nationalisms and its points of view into many discrete and often violent factions, while inequity grows and awareness of it diminishes, the new media come to us as a real hope for the improvement of earth communication, the potential for nothing less than total community communication and the cessation of violence because awareness and understanding ultimately minimize conflict.

It will be possible within fifty years to receive a laser communication at a single terminal within the home enabling the citizen to gather information from radio, teletype, microfilm, telephone, televideo, libraries, satellites, and perhaps even interstellar communication. This is no more fantastic than it was to imagine a hundred years ago that every citizen would have a wire that would connect him to every other citizen—the telephone. Such a vision would have seemed farfetched to men who were resigned to the present physical limitations of their ability to communicate.

However, as long as new technology is developed along the lines of our existing value orientations, the potential of the new media will scarcely be realized and the destructive implications of their features will be explored to the fullest. Guided by the prevailing values, values that have turned the twentieth century into a blood bath, men are very adept at finding the implications of technological control. But they are unable to direct their energies toward the alleviation of the dehumanizing facets of modern life.

What can be done? First, every sane and life-affirming individual must come to know about the new media. Today, ignorance is certainly not bliss: it is a state of alienation. Unfortunately, most information on the new media is either too technical to grasp—an outcome of that Tower of Babel called specialization—or it is enthusiastically mystified by those outside the power structure whose aspiration for community seems less vigorous than their wish for status and elitism. There is a real need for media information to be democratized and made accessible. And the individual must avail himself of openings in accessibility.

But knowledge itself does little to develop individual potency, nor does it create much of an impact on the environment. The informed individual must then become *involved* with the new media. It is here that social change is usually aborted. Sequestered from direct action within the teaching profession, the intelligentsia continually promotes the illusion that information exists only to be passed on. Being aware, however, involves a commitment to action. But professors are not generally doers, and those who act tend to have short academic lives.

The intelligentsia has been made comfortable. Fuller calls specialists the information gatherers for the Old Pirates (and the Old Pirates pay generously for services rendered). Very little that has resulted from recent decades of university life dispels the suggestion that intelligence *per se* is rewarded. In our time, too few are prepared to forsake material rewards for the less tangible value of contribution, especially when contribution is so frequently punished.

Yet as many people as possible must become involved in the new media, and *children* particularly must be able to communicate with these media naturally. This will require the wisdom and commitment of their teachers. The first generation to be acculturated by broadcast television has, now that they are adults, demanded that there be a new television. Children sitting in classrooms today must become acquainted with other new media if they are to be more than passive recipients of programmed fare.

People are motivated to participate in social struggle by a deep-seated feeling of what it is they feel must be changed. A younger generation capable and comfortable with the new media will constitute the greatest force in democratizing and redirecting the uses of the new ways of communicating.

We are finally led to the politics of media; all those who would divorce research, involvement, and information from politics have already assumed their own lack of power. A dehumanized society is not neutral to the forces that would change it. Involvement with the new media will reveal certain imposed limitations. Most of the serious investigation into videotape, mind-expanding drugs, ESP, Kirillian photography, and acupuncture has been done against obstacles created by the institutions of government and industry. If this situation is beginning to change, it is only because men driven by the values of control and exploitation are interested in these phenomena for their use in furthering the effectiveness of existing behaviors.

At this very moment, important political decisions are being made which at a later time will be offered as the "traditional" ways society regulates the new media. It might well be that today's ignorance of media politics will limit the future options for human connection. If there are not sufficient numbers of alert, informed, and vocal media-watchers present now, today's decision will become tomorrow's law. The options of new media will be closed. The best and most obvious example demonstrating the need for sensitive media-watchers is the case of cable relay television. By the time the reader finishes this book he should be aware of the enormous potential of cable television. Cable will create great access to information; it will also greatly assist self-identity, democratic processes, educational environments, and community cohesion. The degree to which we are sensitive and responsive to the emerging regulations and uses of cable will do more to determine the ultimate significance of this communication system than the technological development of cable itself.

Unfortunately, many media-watchers today believe that the technology will transcend all attempts to contain it, that the positive qualities of the new media will be realized inevitably. They believe with Buckminster Fuller that as soon as we realize that there are enough resources to go around and that our present technology will enable us to do more with less—i.e., as soon as the new media create an ecological consciousness—we will set about ending war, preventing widescale poverty and disease, and providing a stable industrial base for countries now lacking one. Then we would see that such change would have been worth all the fortunes that had not been made, all the appliances and products we would not have had the opportunity to buy, and some of the short-term prosperity now associated with war, arms, and defense that would not have been enjoyed.

If the media-watcher believes that, despite regulation, obstacles, and present industrial interests, the media will prevail, he will certainly not be attentive to media politics. As well as media enthusiasts we need media-watchers to enforce media action programs based on human values that will reorder the present priorities. Much of the world today is geared to the maintenance of inequity and the withholding of surplus. Our present values have been based on absurd definitions of "progress," and are reinforced by a crass materialism of endless glut. The new media can either foster a new dynamic consumerism, an electronic package for the old values, or they can serve as a primary communication for the new values that are incarnate within the media themselves. Can there be a choice?

Unlike the prophets of the past who pictured apocalyptic nightmares as the result of divine retribution, our diviners are the ecologists, scientists, and poets who tell us we do not have an indefinite amount of time to continue our ecological self-destruction. Those who speak of the death of the air and ocean, mass famine, lead poisoning, nuclear holocaust, race wars, and of lemmings running to the sea in mass suicide do not base their concerns on the fanciful vision of an angry god, but on statistics, intuitions, and scientific facts.

If there is an apocalyptic message that must be heard, if human society is, in fact, nearing the fail-safe point, it is clear that existing patterns of communication and the present media are sorely inadequate for the communication of *both* the present plight *and* the future alternatives, options and developments that might open a way beyond the present crisis. The new media discussed, evaluated, and *felt* in this book are the tools for the final analysis of an old world and the communication of the birth rites of a new one. Without access to and control over the role these media will play in our lives, we can have only a less hopeful vision of the future.

For some years now I have collected tropical fish. Only recently did I feel sufficiently competent to maintain a marine aquarium. The challenge of collecting salt-water life is infinitely greater than that for fresh water. Though many specialists believe that precise controls on temperature, pH, trace metals, copper, and nitrates are required for the fish, the well-being of the invisible bacteria is supremely important in the chemistry of the fish tank. If the bacteria die, the waste, measured by nitrate counts, will build up to lethal levels.

Last October the bacteria in my tank died. As I gazed into the fish tank, I saw healthy marine specimens happily swimming and enjoying their lives. I was completely unaware that as I looked into the tank all the healthy fish inside were, for practical purposes, already dead. That they died one month later was inevitable and predictable. Had I used a nitrate test to determine whether the conditions of the water had deteriorated, I might have saved the environment and those living things within it. Some argue today that our environment, the planet, is like my doomed home aquarium. Surely, many of our most reputable thinkers have made it patently clear that the conditions for our ultimate demise are advancing along chartable lines. But this feedback is filed under "long-term worries." There are no long-term worries. The new media promises to communicate the feedback telling us that existing values must be altered and to reveal some of the ways a new world conforming to new perceptions can be created.

The new media contain at least the following developments: satellite communication, color television, cable relay television, cassettes, videotape, videotape computer systems, videophones, electrostatic reproduction techniques, laser communication, electronic high-speed printing, electronic learning machines, printing by radio, time-sharing computers, generalized data banks, telepathy, various parapsychological phenomena, holography, biofeedback, and interstellar communication. These new forms of media are also capable of forming innumerably varied hybrid media with each other and with older media like printing, radar, X ray, teletype, and film. Some day in the not too distant future, communication may be comprised of a universal world grid of electricity and energy capable of transformation into countless forms and variations within forms. Thus, the earth itself may be encapsulated by an electric communication atmosphere that encircles it.

I have not attempted to inform the reader of the most current and vital new developments in media. No book can do this. It takes about nine months from submission of manuscript to first printing, and that is too long to reasonably expect to have the last word on anything. Instead, I have distilled from the enormous bulk of writing on the new media strong statements that help acquaint the general reader with them—what their potential is, how they may open avenues for human connection, and what kinds of politics bear on a discussion of them.

the dialectics
of media

Several years ago the playwright Eugene Ionesco wrote down his conviction that "the human condition determines the social condition, and not vice versa." The context for this remark is a discussion of the nature of evil. Is the flaw in the world we each experience accounted for by the imperfections in our social system, or is man's fundamental dissatisfaction with life determined by his relationship to life itself? These are questions of an "existential" nature, arising from an investigation of man's situation in the world.

Perhaps it is a sign of the continuing secularization of society that we do not ask such questions in the 1970s. Our social situation so determines our condition today that we are led to ask different questions, the most pressing of which can be articulated by paraphrasing and changing Ionesco's formulation: "the communications media determine the social condition, and not vice versa." This view, and its antithesis, is one major, perhaps *the* major intellectual debate within our time. Some argue that the new electronic environment will change society; others say that the new communications media will be hopelessly ensnarled by regulations and monopolies. The first view supposes that the ways a society communicates change the society; the opposite position concludes that only a changed society will communicate in changed ways.

In fact, both views are correct: The new media *are* capable of changing societies *and* their potential is greatly undermined by the power structures that determine the uses to which the new media are put. However, the extreme positions should be studied, for they both illuminate the murky middle ground most of us have to live on. To this end I have assembled an artificial debate between Buckminster Fuller and Kingsley Widmer. Widmer, who is an outstanding social critic and too little appreciated by those who prefer their criticism in small doses, argues passionately that most of the electronic environment rhetoric is beside the point, that as long as the media are programmed by the present media decision-makers, *they* will do more of the same, only with less effort. Widmer's essay pulls no punches; he defines the state of the media without the illusion of panaceas. And yet, though Widmer appears to be right, he also seems uninvolved with the media itself. Widmer has a problem in levels of generalization. Usually his kind of analysis, a form of what Hemingway called "crap detecting," has an enduring value. But the new media are exceptional and unique and not just more efficient tools in the hands of the programmers. Sociopolitical analysis must be tempered by the fact that involvement with the media does lead to certain discoveries that are genuine, i.e., not known by conventional predication. Widmer's essay does much to elucidate facets of the media problem; but while it contains strong perceptions, it is not definitive.

One might say that Widmer is so acquainted with our present and past that he cannot accept the idea that our future might not derive from them. On the opposite pole is Buckminster Fuller, who believes that, in fact, the new media, and new technology generally, have made it possible to disengage ourselves from our present and invalidate our past.

Among other things, he is a man who has shown us that the closer we are to a subject the less we know about it, that the more detached our perspective, the greater the inclination of the mind (not the brain) to achieve metaphysical insights. He is, of course, an architect, designer, and scientist. But more significant, I suspect, for thousands of passionate admirers, is that he is a master storyteller of the new consciousness, a wizard who ferments analogy and logic, and combines metaphors of man, nature, and universe into a more coherent and more human vision of planet earth.

Fuller is orbiting somewhere in intellectual space, radiating celestial comprehension from the special vantage point of genius, surveying the human condition with undisturbed ego. Possessing wit, brilliance, and a flexible intuition, he wishes earnestly, if somewhat naïvely, that we should all realize that we are not each other's enemy, that there is enough to go around in the world, that man's technology has opened the door to abundance and happiness, that our present ways of thinking work against our own well-being, and that once we have perceived this we should think differently.

Thus, Fuller, in his way, is a cosmological moralist. If men believed what Fuller believes and acted on what they believed, his analysis would be absolutely correct. A world of Buckminster Fuller's would be a world of sharing, of planning, of the greatest human needs receiving the greatest human attention. But it is, Kingsley Widmer would remind us, not Buckminster Fuller's world.

A moralist is one who argues a value system in the face of its denial. If Fuller is to be taken as a designer, then one would have to say that his design is inappropriate to the human species. Fuller's vision of the future is only one of many we might develop *if we believed* we could create our future. Most of mankind does not. The man who does not believe he can create his future is less inclined to try.

Fuller believes that we now have at our disposal the means to create worldwide abundance. He interprets the efforts to maintain divisions between the haves and the have-nots as a vestigial mentality, the legacy of an older time when the Darwinian and Malthusian views of scarcity may have been correct. But believing they are no longer correct, Fuller passionately argues that we must redirect our consciousness. To help show us that abundance is achievable, he has written numerous articles and books, invented the geodesic dome, and has begun to compile an inventory of the world's resources as well as the world game, which is designed to assist mankind in making the transition.

Though Fuller acknowledges the presence of men who do not believe we can have abundance, he does not adequately deal with those who believe that we could have abundance but who still do not opt for it. This man of good (for Buckminster Fuller is a good man) has not yet come to terms with the question of evil. By assuming that destructive acts come from mentalities that believe war, exploitation, and the division between rich and poor are needed for survival, he also assumes that, once shown abundance is possible, men will cast off their competitive, destructive, greedy urges and choose to live in harmony. But did Iago worm his way into the psyche of Othello because he wanted Desdemona?

Unlike most of the intelligentsia, Fuller places his emphasis on mind, not brain. Fuller argues that unless we choose for the mind, and thereby discover its many powers, we will be obliterated. If we do choose for the mind, if we enable the metaphysical to overcome the physical, we will have utopia. The dilemma that Fuller both presents and is somewhat trapped by is that the human condition is not and has never been the exclusive outcome of what men have construed as reasonable. One cannot reasonably account for several thousand years of human dominance, hierarchy, and violence with the explanation that this is what earlier humans thought they needed to do. Fuller emerges as a true moralist when he argues that we *must* change our orientation, values, and consciousness if we are to escape oblivion.

At first the fact that Fuller writes much of his thoughts as poetry might seem unclear. However, if we think of him as a moralist who writes a poetry of immense beauty within the scope of his vision, we can better define how he serves us and the lasting impact of his contribution. For if he too easily dismisses the world that Widmer is mired in, he lingers in a vision of a new world, one which postulates a humanity far more in tune with universal harmony and far more equipped to live on the planet and in the cosmos than the men of limited vision who now direct the misuse of resources.

Those of us who share his vision, but do not believe that others will necessarily choose to do so, are inspired by his dream of human community and are aghast at the efforts of those around us who would perpetuate inequity. Fuller may be postpolitical, as so many of his youthful followers are, but the world itself seems quite willing to lose a few devotees from its ongoing program of political perpetuity. If Fuller's vision does acquire the means to put values into action, then a very desperate struggle may ensue that will result in either utopia or oblivion.

Fuller believes that all men are capable of logic and reason, that if they could realize that inequity has no justification, they would forsake the politicians and seek to create a new world. Thus, from his point of view, the task before mankind is partly an educational one. Though the probabilities of finding enough teachers for this task are slight, and though infusing the educational system or an alternative one with freedom will be difficult, all great ideas, he believes, have transcended the obstacles to them.

One disagrees with Fuller without disagreeing. He is brilliant and right. But when one comes to put values in action, his usefulness diminishes. He has a truth, but not the way to the truth. Thus, he ends *Operating Manual for Spaceship Earth* with: "So, planners, architects, and engineers, take the initiative. Go to work, and above all co-operate and don't hold back on one another or try to gain at the expense of another."

Who is he talking to? Though I share his vision of that other world we have yet to create, the way to that world remains uncertain. Fuller designs out of the human condition the benign impact of absurdity itself. History is the outcome of human choice, and human choice may be capricious. Thus, his philosophy leads to utopia or oblivion, whereas history itself may offer a less dramatic continuum of diminished values and forsaken lives. I think we will not have utopia, but more cause for optimism; I think we will not have oblivion, but much more human decay. We will move toward a Renaissance in the twenty-first century or a Dark Ages. We will come to know better the vision of moralist Fuller, or the world so precisely mapped by Widmer; but in any case, we will be able to determine the outcome by the degree of importance we give to the new media, and by our commitment to ensuring that their value is maximized.

Chapter 1

utopia
or oblivion

R. Buckminster Fuller

Astronauts, aviators, mariners, submariners, and people of all countries use and appreciate tiny transistors, because transistors do so much more, so much more reliably with so much less. So also do a myriad of invisible alloys, chemical and electromagnetic devices accomplish much more with less.

The development of these globally interacting, invisibly operating inventions was not organized as a benevolent world revolution by anyone. But their integrating and interacceleratingly regenerative more-with-lessing all together constitute a revolution which is found to be politically welcome the world around. Computers, TV's, and plastics, as superficial manifest of the invisible doings, are apparently wanted everywhere.

The centuries' long only subconscious more-with-lessing is only now entering human consciousness as constituting a unified world revolution—as inexorable and transcendental to man's will as is an earthquake. Some speak of the revolution as "the impact of technology on society," others as "automation." Everywhere people are aware of its portentousness. Few think of it correctly as "invisible more-with-lessing," the scientific description for which is "progressive ephemeralization"—99% of humanity look upon it only as more-with-more and more again.

To turn the heretofore only subconsciously regenerative more-of-every-advantage with less-of-every-resource revolution to highest human benefit in the shortest time with the most pleasure and satisfaction and with the least effort, pain, or rupture for all has become the conscious focus of a world-around university students' coordinated research. Whether this particular initiative will persist and be successful is unpredictable. But its occurrence and circumstances provide a significant case history for it brings the generalized problem into sharp, wide-angle-lensed, maximum depth-of-field focus. As such it is probably the prototype exploration in how to make the world work satisfactorily for all.

Identified as the Design Science Decade, the world students' ten-year plan is divided into five evolutionary stages of two years each. Stage one was on exhibit in the Tuileries Gardens in Paris, France, for the first ten days of July, 1965 (under the auspices of the International Union of Architects' Eighth World Congress). It confronted the world with the basic facts which led the students to the research conclusion that human survival apparently depends upon an immediate, consciously coordinated, world-around, computerized research marshalling and inception of the theoretically required additional inventions and industrial network integrations for the swiftest attainment and maintenance of physical success of all humanity.

Fortunately, say the students, such invention initiative does not derive from political debate or bureaucratic licensing. The license comes only from the blue sky of the inventor's intellect. No one licensed the inventors of the airplane, telephone, electric light, and radio to go to work. It took only five men to invent these world-transforming developments. Herein lies the potentially swift effectiveness of the world student research revolution. . . .

The world students' design-science initiative has no precedent. All the conditions essential to its precipitation have never before coexisted. It is the constructive outgrowth of the world-around students' ever-more-logical dissatisfaction with the inadequacy of yesterday's theories and practices to cope with today's problems and potentials. Their highly intuitive and not always clearly conceived dissatisfaction is frequently articulated only in protests over local regulations, or the right to be heard. Sometimes, in civil-rights movements, the students' spirit discloses superb courage and dedication to human justice. Sometimes—in wanton outbursts of indiscriminate disdain of the ineptness of all that is "old"—it may break windows and noses. Typical of the milder, organized protests was the recent University of California students' Berkeley rebellion.

The issues are often confused because of political tampering. It is easy for skilled operators of opposing world ideologies to surreptitiously exploit the universally persistent, intuitive discontent among their adversaries' youth by derring-do teasing in their respective directions.

Born utterly helpless, and gaining independent competence only slowly, youth's reflexes are preconditioned to expect some older authority to be responsible for its welfare. Youth assumes that the political authority is a public parent. When dissatisfied, youth protests to the authorities, assuming the authorities can, if they wish, make everything satisfactory. Often, the "authority" lacks such capability. The problems are usually beyond the scope of local authority. They demand world peace. The Mayor of Kankakee has no such capability.

The present university youth are World War II's babies, many born with their fathers away at war. Many were tended by group babysitters as their mothers worked in munitions factories. The present university students are also the first humans to be reared by the third parent—*television*—which has given them hourly news of world events. Unlike any previous generations, the students think "world." They will settle for nothing less than justice and physical advantage for all, everywhere around earth.

The third parent also taught them that no invention barriers are insurmountable to science and technology. They were born into a transoceanic, air-traveling world. The atom bomb is their birthmark. In their fourth year of life the giant transistorized computers began commercial operation. When the students were aged 9, men climbed to the peak of Mount Everest. When 10, they were immunized against polio. As they reached 12 years, the Russians' unmanned rocket Sputnik orbited the earth every hour and a half, and the first civilian nuclear reactor went into operation as an electric power-generating station. When the students were aged 13, the U.S. atomic-powered submarine *Nautilus* went from the Pacific to the Atlantic submerged below the north polar ice. In their four-teenth year, the Russians' unmanned rocket photographed the far side of the moon and returned to earth. When they were 15, the U.S. bathyscaphe took man safely to photograph the bottom of the Pacific Ocean's deepest hole. In their sixteenth year, a Russian orbited earth in a rocket. As they reached 17, the DNA genetic code for the control of the design of all life was discovered.

The students know that man can do anything he wants. However, they see world officialdom investing the world's highest capabilities only in race suicide springboards. Finding their own political demonstrations for peace or their outright revolutions leading only toward further war, a few pioneers amongst the world students have joined up objectively with the heretofore only subjectively experienced do-more-with-less design-science revolution. The students are applying general systems theory to comprehend and to utilize the accelerating invention revolution as the swiftest and only fundamental means of attaining world peace with both physical success and moral justice for all. . . .

No exclusively political act of any political system can make the world's resources take care of more than 44% of humanity.

Despite the foregoing constant increase in human population and constant decrease of metals per person, between 1900 and 1965 the number of people attaining physical success as full-time participants in the highest standard of living progressively developed by world industrialization—a personal standard of living and health superior to that ever enjoyed by any pre-20th-century monarch—rose steadily from less than 1% to 40% of all living humanity.

The 40% of humanity surprisingly grown successful, despite constantly diminishing physical resources per capita, can only be explained by the doing-more-with-less invention revolution.

The success cannot be attributed to any political doctrine. It has flourished equally under opposing ideologies.

Take away the energy-distribution networks and the industrial machinery from America, Russia, and all the worlds' industrialized countries and within six months over two billion swiftly and painfully deteriorating people will starve to death.

Take away the politicians, all the ideologies and their professional protagonists from those same countries and leave them their present energy networks, industrial machinery, routine production and distribution personnel and no more humans will starve nor be afflicted in health than at present.

Why has mankind failed to perceive, understand, and respond logically to the significance of this situation? The answer is complex. But it needs answering. That will take some paragraphs. If it is to be consciously solved by man it will have to be understood well enough to be properly stated. It is the students' working assumption that "a problem adequately stated is a problem well on its way to being solved."

The problem consists of such powerfully conditioned human reflexes as laissez-faire, induced by nature's "built-in," instinctive, "game-playing" drives which are subconsciously operative in all living creatures, by which—often in lieu of intellect, they only inadvertently and unintentionally provide vital support of one another—as for instance do all the mammals respire all the vegetation's vitally required carbon dioxide, while all vegetation respires all the mammals' vitally required oxygen; or as do the honey-hunting bees inadvertently fertilize the growth of flowers with their pollen-dusting tails. It is only by the integrated coordination of myriads upon myriads of unconsciously performed inadvertencies of such "game-playing" drives that nature is able to accomplish the comprehensive ecological and metabolic regeneration of life on earth. . . .

The public's vast ignorance of either the comprehensive or particular nature of original undertakings in technical development has been almost certified by national-defense secrecy. Ninety-nine percent of the original more-with-less invention revolution has been subsidized by the weapons programs of the major nations. Up to World War I all the drawings and calculations of all the world's navies' ships were methodically destroyed as soon as each ship was built, up to which moment they were the most carefully guarded of history's secrets.

During the first half century of the airplane, the major sovereign powers poured $2½ trillion directly and indirectly into aircraft development as the new supreme weapon. Now in one-third that time the world nations have again appropriated almost as much capability wealth for the development of the atomic-headed rocketry and space race, for supreme control of the earth and its surrounding portion of the universe.

Most central to all the remote controlled more-with-lessing of moon-landed rockets and ocean bottom exploring are the swiftly multiplying transistorized electronic computers, one of which can now, in one minute, print-out the solution to a problem which a decade ago would have taken two years to accomplish by the combined efforts of all those educated on earth to calculate. Little wonder that 99% of humanity are left millenniums behind, innocently and innocuously preoccupied in playing yesterday's irrelevant game of "everyday" serious "business," "politics," and "education."

Twenty-five years after the original, secretly developed doing-only-more-killing-with-less-material-and-work-per-death as potentially realized in weapons and weapons-production technology—the, only inadvertently, *generalized do-more-with-less capabilities*—of the tools-to-make-tools, that finally make the special tools called "weapons"—99% of which tooling could also make peaceful products— are secondhanded into the domestic economics of world man to provide more life with less effort. But this ultimate life-support upgrading occurs only after the prime weapon contractors' respective weapons contracts expire and only as a result of the obsolescence of their respective weaponry end-products.

While different political ideologies, as with the different languages and customs as yet operative in yesterday's pirate-decreed and natural-barrier-divided lands, are useful in organizing mankind's employment of the ever-swiftly improving, multiplying, and integrating industrial-tool network of the invention revolution, by-producted from the weaponry-focused economies, it is becoming increasingly visible to ever more people that the industrial network will soon integrate society into a "one-town world" obliterating all national divisions of earth people, invented by the top pirates' competitive-ambition strategies.

It is also increasingly clear to even more people that the fundamental and highest priority responsibility for man's interim-survival success on this little sun-orbiting spaceship, *Earth*, does not fall directly within the problem-solving capabilities of political theory, nor with the results obtainable by politics' ultimately greatest lever

—war—hot, subversive, cool, or cold. *Either war is obsolete, or men are. . . .*

It comes to those who discover it, all round the world, as a dismaying shock to realize that continuation of the weapons race and of cold and hot warring is motivated only by intramural party fears of local political disasters. The world's political fate does not rest with leaders at the summit, expressing the will of world people, but with the local ambitions and fears of lower-echelon political machines, within the major weapons-possessing nations, whose vacillation is accompanied by an increasing spread of the atomic-weapons-possessing nations whose respective internal politics will forever frustrate disarmament by political initiative. All political machine professionals of all political states will always oppose loss of sovereignty for their own state. Solution of the impasse, if it comes at all, must clearly come from other than political initiative.

It is true, the world university students point out, that throughout all history up to now man has been faced with not enough to go around; not even for the survival of more than a small minority. It has always been—you or me. Swift you-or-me by the sword or gun has often been preferable to slow death by slum rot or slavery. The direct and conscious design-science revolution backed by the students can and may, by production of enough for all, accomplish elimination of the lethal you-or-me dictum and its political bias support.

Now, for the first time in history, employing its literary voices, world society can give design science its popularly mandated priority over political initiative with realistic hope as the impelling motivation. As 100% of humanity achieves, or nears, physical-survival success, past history's seemingly inexorable reason for war (not enough for both of us) will have been eliminated.

The students argue that if they can make man conscious of his design-revolution potential, and of the feasible and practical means of its accomplishment—the probability of pushing the annihilation button will be diminished from "critical" to "remote" status.

It seems apparent to students that—for whatever functional purposes man has been included in the design of the universe— nature has been, and continues to be, intent upon mankind's survival in his most physically successful and intellectually useful condition, wherefore, in view of man's historically vast ignorance and fear, nature has employed those predominant "game-motivating" negatives to impel him unconscious, even as she impelled him through the womb, toward this moment of dawning awareness of realistic hope and birth of his responsibility and intellectual initiative. The inadvertent doing-more-with-less as a by-product of the weaponry race seems, retrospectively, to have been nature's trick for developing man's highest potential, while also saving him from his own shortsighted "game-playing" ignorance.

It is inconceivable that one man, one party, one nation, or even a world congress of all mankind's representatives meeting a century ago (1865)—when a million dollars was an almost incredible sum, could have had the vision, logic, and courage to elect to invest $5 trillion in the invention and development of the then uninvented and economically unanticipated telephone; electric light; radio; airplane; jet and rocket flight; nuclear reactor; flight into space; world-around television; elimination of both bacterial and virus diseases; discovery and isolation of 60 additional chemical elements and their electrons, and nuclear components; and the genetic code; together with the ten million additional, mutually interadvantaging technical inventions and discoveries which have occurred in the last century; plus development of industrial mass production and its progressive industrial-production-capacity-geared accrediting of the paper-financed mass-consumption industry; tripling of human longevity and the support of three times as many people on earth, half of them at standards of living better than any king has ever known. Those who suggest that it might all have developed peacefully and purposefully through a shift in political doctrine are as unrealistic as are those who now think that the old public laissez-faire and political-initiative-only patterns can continue without man's annihilating himself; as are those who cannot see that the world students have found a first tiny view of a realistically hopeful blue-sky future. . . .

Science and engineering say the design science's peaceful accomplishment of 100% industrialization and its comprehensively bounteous support of man is eminently feasible. It is feasible because the world's economy is now operating at the appalling low overall mechanical efficiency level at which only 4% of the energy consumed is realized as effective work. Reciprocating engines are 15%, turbines 30%, jet engines 65% efficient. Efficiencies of 72% in atomic reactors—employing their by-product heat in desalination—and up to 80% in fuel cells are now everyday design realities. Increasing the overall mechanical efficiency of the world's prime movers and machinery to only 10% from the present 4% will result in 100% of mankind being benefited by higher living standards than the present highest.

In addition to the world students' reorientation of the public from prime dependence on politics to prime dependence upon design science, there are now in evidence several other hopeful and highly realistic trends toward elimination of the political impasse to be accomplished by accelerating the more-with-lessing to the advantage of all men. Completion of the ultrahigh-voltage world network integration of electrical-energy distribution, under the Bering Straits, which is now clearly possible well within the 20-year trend, will automatically increase the world energy efficiency to an overall of 20%. This energy-distributing network linking the day and night hemispheres of earth will reduce the local standby power losses by 25%. The staggering economical advantage accruing to both public and private sectors has thus far caused both to join unreservedly in its development. The decisions of both public and private sectors to subscribe to their mutual interoperation was never taken as a consequence of interpersuasion by one another or of victory of one over the other. The persuasion came exclusively from the unbiased calculations of computers. The machine showed both sides that they would each profit beyond previous dreams by "integration." The computers will play a swiftly increasing, dominant role in the decisions of men—leading him away from "policy" or political impasse and toward total physical success.

Because energy is wealth, the integrating world network means access of all humanity everywhere to the total operative commonwealth of earth.

Wealth cannot alter yesterday. It can only alter today and tomorrow.

Multiplication of wealth began when man stepped on the long end of a log lying across another log with its short end under another big log, and he saw the big log, which was too heavy for him to lift with his muscles, lifted easily by gravity pulling his minuscule weight against the high-advantage arm of the lever. When man fastened a set of levers radially around the hub of a wheel and put the wheel under a waterfall and connected the wheel with a grinding mill, he learned to stand aside from the work and, gaining perspective, to use his brain to rearrange energy patterns to do more, and more fundamental, man-advantaging work.

Man found that the vast *associative* (gravity, matter) and *dissociative* (radiation) *energy patternings* of universe can be harnessed, shunted, and valved by man to impinge on levers and trains of gears ad infinitum.

Man is now learning through the repeated lessons of experimental science that wealth is explicitly the organized and operative tool and energy capability to sustain his forward metabolic regeneration; to protect him physically; to increase his knowledge and degrees of freedom while decreasing his interfrustrations. Wealth, he finds, is inherently regenerative. Experimentally demonstrated wealth is: energy compounded with intellect's knowhow.

Science's Law of Conservation of Energy states that "energy cannot be created or destroyed." The *first constituent* of wealth—energy—is therefore irreducible. Sciences states that the entire physical universe is ENERGY. $E = Mc^2$.

Every time man uses the second constituent of wealth—his knowhow—this intellectual resource automatically increases.

Energy cannot decrease. Knowhow can only increase.

It is therefore scientifically clear that wealth which combines energy and intellect can only increase, and that wealth can increase only with use and that wealth increases as fast as it is used. The faster-the-more! Those are the facts of science. Those are the facts of life.

The students know that they can generate more wealth through their cooperative initiative than in competition with each other. Cooperation generates commonwealth. They need not be concerned about "making a living" for themselves. By dedicating themselves to research in "how to make the world work for all in the shortest possible time" they will be realizing the only living now possible which is for all or none. . . .

Man's reflexes are conditioned to brush aside that statement on the grounds that "Utopia" has become synonymous with the "unrealistic" or "impossible." This is because the many past attempts to establish Utopias all failed. The fact is that all past at-

tempts were unrealistic before they started. All the historical Utopian attempts occurred when it was assumed that Malthus was right
and that there never would be enough physical resources for more
than 1% of humans to live out their potential fourscore and ten
years in comfort; nor for more than one ten-thousandth of 1% to
live it out in precarious luxury as well as comfort; nor for any to
live out their full span in health, safety, comfort, luxury, good conscience, and happiness. The latter would, of course, be the minimum
requirements for everybody in the establishment of Utopia. That
is why their attempts were "unrealistic" in the light of their working knowledge that those conditions could not then be met or even
dreamed of.

It was said at that time that "man cannot lift himself up by
his bootstraps." No one thought in the terms of doing-more-with-
less. No Utopians thought of airplanes as a possible reality, not
in terms of aircraft engines multiplying thousandfold in power
while simultaneously reducing their engine and airframe weights
per horsepower by 99%. No one thought of communications going
from wire to wireless with enormous gains in distance accomplished
per unit of invested materials, as well as a manifold reduction of
weight and energy per each frequency-tuned message circuit; none
thought of a 1/10-ton Telstar satellite outperforming 75,000 tons
of transatlantic cable.

The great transformation of man's physical capabilities by
scientific industrialization, which alone could provide the physical
environment and harnessed energy adequate and essential to a
Utopian level of metabolic-regeneration success for all humanity
had neither occurred nor even been as yet scientifically conceived.
As so far experienced, in their day, the would-be Utopians could
reasonably think, for instance, of bigger, more fireproof, more
bow-and-arrow-proof stone or brick walls instead of wood. They
could think of common austerity. They could think of having more
cows, or more acres, but experience, until then, gave them no
thoughts of the doing-more-with-less science and technology revolution. Some cows gave more milk than others as some men were taller
than others. There was good or bad luck. There was mystical blessed-
ness or confoundment.

Not only did all the attempts to establish Utopias occur pre-
maturely (in respect of technological capability to establish and

maintain any bacteria- and virus-immune, hungerless, travel any-where Utopias), but all of the would-be Utopians disdained all the early manifestations of industrialization as "unnatural, stereotyped, and obnoxiously sterile." The would-be Utopians, therefore, attempted only metaphysical and ideological transformations of man's nature—unwitting any possible alternatives. It was then unthinkable that there might soon develop a full capability to satisfactorily transform the physical energy events and material structure of the environment—not by altering man, but by helping him to become literate and to use his innate cerebral capabilities, and thereby to at least achieve man's physical survival at a Utopianly successful level.

All the attempts to establish Utopias were not only premature and misconceived, but they were also exclusive. Small groups of humanity withdrew from and forsook the welfare of the balance of humanity. Utopia must be, inherently, for all or none. A minority's knowledge that the majority of humanity suffers and deteriorates while only the minority prospers would never permit a Utopian degree of contentment of the all-powerful subconscious reflexing of the human brain. In the far from Utopianly idealistic lives of history's "aristocratic" minorities, which were alone supportable by the known means and resource effectiveness of the preindustrial era, attempts were made by the successful minority to exclude thoughts of humanity's generally inexorable suffering by inventing "important" cultural preoccupations. However, dilettantism, sports, banquets, art patronage, flirtations, dueling, intrigue, and war failed to appease the subconscious reflexing of kings' and courtiers' brains. Their lopsided and twilighted conscience, therefore, imposed a code of affected blindness. This irrationality was propped up by an assumption of divine wisdom having placed a few in preposterous survival advantage over the many because of their superior wisdom, culture, and capability to fight for the less fortunate.

As a consequence, the poor illiterate masses built their churches and prayed that they and theirs be given strength to endure life, and that they be blessed—"blessed" means "wounded"—and possibly escape by death from unendurable life to a dreamed-of good life thereafter. All this is now changed, not because man has changed, but because man has found that he is endowed with a powerful brain which has found out what a few of the invisible principles operative in physical universe can do. But universe having permitted him to discover his intellectual effectiveness as well as some of universe's riches, and thus to participate consciously as well as only subconsciously in universal evolution, will now require him to use his intellect directly and effectively. Success or failure is now all of humanity's responsibility.

The present top-priority world problem to be solved may be summarized as how to triple, swiftly, safely, and satisfyingly, the overall performances per kilos, kilowatts, and man-hours of the world's comprehensively invested resources of elements, energy, time, and intelligence. To do so will render those resources—which at the present uncoordinated, happenstance, design level can support only 44% of humanity—capable of supporting 100% of humanity's increasing population at higher standards of living than any human minority or single individual has ever known or dreamed of and will thus eliminate the cause of war and its weapons' frustrating diversion of productivity from the support of all mankind.

Because politicians will not dare to stop politicking, and because income-supported individuals will not risk loss of their incomes, and because the wage-earning world will not dare to drop its income-producing activity to promulgate the design-science achievement, it can only be undertaken by the more or less freewheeling student world. If the student handling of its initiative is well done, then in the progressively accelerating emergencies of human society, the significance of the students' initiative will loom into increasing prominence as their design inventions are put to work, soon in sufficient degree to persuade the wage-earning adults to transfer their efforts to support the student initiative. If this occurs within the next decade, man may succeed in his continuance upon earth. Because of the students' intuition and youth, the chances are good!

. . . Let us, too, at least give ourselves a chance to vote to commit ourselves earnestly for the Design Science Decade approach to attaining Utopia. This moment of realization that it soon must be Utopia or Oblivion coincides exactly with the discovery by man that for the first time in history Utopia is, at least, physically possible of human attainment.

Chapter 2

sensibility under technocracy: reflections on the culture of processed communications

Kingsley Widmer

Writing in an earlier phase of the "communications explosion," in an era of the burgeoning of American newspapers, Henry David Thoreau defiantly asserted that he would have nothing to do with the weekly "news." Even in rural New England in the first half of the nineteenth century that sounded a bit odd, so Thoreau went on to explain that what passed for "news" rarely achieved that quality and, besides, was mostly irrelevant, redundant and distracting. That has been the usual view of the sage. Two millennia earlier, Chuang-Tzu suggested that the wise man might be awakened each morning by a crowing cock in the next village yet never bother to find out what was happening a cock's crow away. The Taoist and Transcendentalist taste in media, and such astute perceptions about what passes for news, may still be valid. But the claims to autonomy of Chuang-Tzu and Thoreau often can't be extended into our time. Contemporary Western man's media environment is ubiquitous, and the news and the crowing cocks will not keep their distance.

Their signs and sounds—imprinted, xeroxed, neoned, transistorized—pervade our villages and Waldens as well as our cities. Few can long escape the communications explosion and its shrapnel of labels, ads, directions, pop tunes and news. Shattered images and

"Sensibility Under Technocracy: Reflections on the Culture of Processed Communications," by Kingsley Widmer (California State University, San Diego). From *Arts in Society*, vol. 9 (Summer–Fall 1972). Abbreviated version © 1973 by Kingsley Widmer. Reprinted by permission of the author and publisher.

other fragments of processed ideology will surely riddle almost everyone's consciousness. We may choose not to communicate but we shall be communicated with, no matter what, short of complete catatonia. Our sensibilities have to be pocked warscapes of the media assault.

"News," rather more than ideas or art or enterainment, provides the mainline justifications for our technological media. The priority of the whole panoply of our amazing equipment, from ballpoint pocket pens to computerized television networks, rests, they say, on "informational utility." Obvious—or is it? News-information, as commonly defined, actually plays but a small part, providing less than thirty percent of most daily newspapers, less than ten percent of most daily broadcasting, and similarly small proportions in books and periodicals. We might, of course, metaphorically extend "news" to include commercials, top-forty pop records, sports, the standardized fantasies called media "entertainment," the pseudo-events of celebritydom and the pseudo-truths of officialdom. But by any reasonable calculus, most of this serves, at best, as organized misinformation, when it is not, under spurious claims of an impossible "objectivity," sheer indoctrination.

The pertinent understanding of contemporary media can hardly accept the "informational" camouflage. Cast a cold eye on the ways most people relate to the media "news." They seem to only half-listen to the hourly radio "news spot," disassociatedly scan the surreal jumble of newspaper pages, mesmerize themselves with the half-hour television news "program." As with the responses to most ads and entertainments, consciousness seems to be moving in some strange realm of epiphenomenalism based in a quite different reality. Taking in "the news" seems to be rather more ritualistic than informational.

News-as-ritual may be confirmed by the aesthetics of news presentation—the pretentious formats with the fracturing headlines, the shamanistic announcers, the portentous music and visuals, and the revealingly narcissistic emphasis. Not the world reported on but the *process* itself becomes the crucial experience. The processing-programming style consumes all, merging every reality into the arbitrarily delimited package, equalizing the sporting game and the genocidal war, a commercial quip and a social philosophy, the trivial and the tragic. Sometimes skillfully, of course—grandiloquent packaging may be the ultimate American art. But "informing" can hardly describe its purposes or effects.

Look, too, at media news in terms of its least varying contents. Local weather reports, for example, come out as comic interludes on television, a mixture of weak joke and jargon and visual display—of little real concern to most urbanized viewers yet seemingly essential to the packaging. Similarly with "sports reports," specialized yet almost never analytic, at once arcane and simple-minded. That is just another definition of ritual style. Some recent studies suggest that many people follow the sports "scores" who do not otherwise relate to the athletic activity and who understand few of its nuances. One finds similar response in most mass religious practices. The ceremonial function appears equally strong in those most rococo sections of the "news service"—the decorum-rigid "press conference," the fatuously fractured and controlled "interview," and the other quaintly decorative "features." More generally, "content analysis" of media "news shows" reveals a tremendous redundancy combined with a low level of information, and even lower levels of analysis and interpretation. Rationality is not central to such experiences.

As I see them—and myself—the audience responds to media information in devotee fashion, piously and repetitively going through the normative reading, listening and viewing of the same events over and over again at the same times in the same ways. The media material, like the hormone-injected salt mush for animal forced-fattening, simultaneously feeds and increases the ritual hunger. Surely the media do impart some information and a certain, albeit often misleading, sense of the world, just as more ancient rituals impart some metaphysical dogma and certain, albeit often misleading, solace from the world. All such rituals serve to confirm accepted and official views of reality, re-sanctifying the sanctified. No doubt such ritualization seems essential in what many feel to be an acceleratingly complex and confusing world. Disorder requires more sanctioning and solacing description than does order, which is to say that it requires more misdescription. Thus the "informational utility" of our technological communications largely rests in rituals of misinformation. And thus it is not at all odd that media consumption tends to inverse relation to understanding. The audience responds obsessionally rather than critically, less learning of and interpreting reality than exorcising and ceremonializing the threatening world.

Nor is this confined to the obvious public media. Our other controlling institutions, such as schools and universities and corporate bureaucracies, also ritually process us with their burgeoning "communications." Institutional programming now packages information and entertainment in a mystification of what is being done, and not done, creating a mythology of need and acceptance. At many levels, communication-rituals aim to control our sensibilities.

When electronic devotees attempt to identify teleculture's favored and distinctive forms, they usually put "news" first, then, variously, sports events or old movies or talk-shows. All but that last arrive as re-runs of other media. Only the talk-show seems to have achieved a distinctive popular form, and therefore we may take its characteristics as basic revelation of the medium. Even at its most ambitious, the talk-show presents less art than the artistic personality as its surrogate. The intellectual, in his or her rare appearances, becomes a spot performer between commercials. The popular adventurer or eccentric appears incongruously and stutteringly disconnected from their realities. The sexologist or demographer or mild dissenter (no others allowed) or other wiseman must operate as polite quipster to the dominant show-biz entertainers. Homogenized into a synthetically theatrical time and space, artist, intellectual, adventurer, expert and personality become props in a rigid and restrictive commercial-ceremonial package. All authentic persons thus become denatured and can only ritualistically parody themselves and their meanings. The undercutting commercialism, the mechanical timing (so experience rarely finds an organic length), the ornate arranging (so that artificiality overcomes any possible substance), the show-business professionalization (so that flashy grossness and ignorant narcissism tone all), the entertainment stylization (so that decorous amusement limits seriousness—in an hysterical refusal of all meaning, the maestros giggle constantly at nothing), this ritual processing is the art of it all, and just about all the art of it.

Is all this the result of bad people and bad purposes controlling the media? Certainly mass broadcasting and publishing are primarily devoted to exploitation and domination, and the hierophants of the media may be, as a group, shrewdly stupid and dully corrupt. Still, the technocommunications themselves must have more than an incremental role in this. Granted: business is still business; the absolutistic state operates in communications, too, on its own power imperatives; and the technocommunications are used by business, government, and other institutions, for their own social and ideological dominations. Technologists, as such, neither rule nor program our communications. Naivete about social controls and institutional imperatives makes most futurist writings on the media rather silly. Technological mystagogues, such as Buckminster Fuller and Marshall McLuhan, quite ignore the controlling functions of the media as well as their irrational roles in mythologizing reality and ritualizing responses. Unless radical social and cultural reorderings take place, we can expect future technocommunications to considerably serve the doctrines and dominations of the past.

Yet, as the communications theorists love to point out, technocommunications "enlarge exponentially." So does their "information." From an arithmetic base we get a geometric expansion. As with population, technocommunications "explode." Many things get blown up by the accelerating quantative change, art and humane discourse among them. The means will master the messages, the expansive communications will take over and determine much of what is to be communicated. Technocommunications develop by selectively serving social and ideological powers—the state, corporate orders, certain dubious "elites," and their pre-technological views— but the servants become so big the masters end in thrall to them.

In such technocracy, art tends to lose many of its past purposes—representation, the maintenance of craft, the creation of autonomous sensibility. Early modernist literary intellectuals and social theorists blamed "the decline in aesthetic and moral taste" on the media appealing to "uncultivated audiences," the newspapers and novels of the materialistic middle-class and, later, the semi-literate urban masses. A great tradition of anti-industrial and anti-bourgeoisie critics and artists developed theories of "mass culture" for a mass society. They gave us brilliant dystopian prophecies, as with those of Zamiatin in *We* (the forerunner of *Brave New World* and *1984*) in which an authoritarian "Benefactor" uses all the methods of technological communications, plus surgical "fantisectomy" to remove the rebellious individual imagination, and thereby obtains a complete control of human sensibility in the ultimate religion of robotized power. It remains possible but perhaps more likely we face a broader technological-social control and its shorting-out of full human sensibility and responsiveness. Uncontrollable by humane intelligence and responsive community, our self-aggrandizing technocommunications must lack most moral and aesthetic qualities. As the ancient philosophers would say, "it is not of their nature." So, too, with bureaucratic paper, that dark ex-forest hiding us from ourselves. It lacks most art and sensitivity, not to mention literacy and sense, and probably, in its quantity and function, cannot be otherwise. From sheer technique and mass, technocommunications may impose their own qualities, or lack of them. Some are good, in the senses of useful and convenient and pleasant. But the technical and quantative responses also bleed into other things. For instance, most scientific and humanistic scholars despairingly comment on the impossibility of "keeping up with the literature in the field." Whether one's concern be with genetic experiments, neolithic artifacts, explications of romantic poetry, applications of microwaves, or research on the mass media, the information on the subject seems unmanageable. Is this the result of "real" and "new" knowledge, or the residue of the communications processing? In the fields in which I can judge, the "knowledge explosion" is, like media "news," largely not new and, to echo Thoreau, seems irrelevant, redundant and distracting. A noted scientist tells me that "about eighty percent of the literature in my field is nonsense"; in my own fields I would have to propose a higher percentage and stronger language. Yet we seem, too, caught in its ritual compulsions.

The information explosion also encourages some new "laws" of information handling which apply to scholarship as well as to bureaucratic communications and the mass media. Much information must be treated as if it were not real, only self-serving. Indeed, when one scans through the latest pile of journals, or plows through yet another committee report, or watches an evening of TV, he may intentionally relate to the material for satiation of sensibility or ritual avoidance of something else, including the ironic pleasures of being inundated with nonsense. A second law might be that as information increases disproportionately so will pervasive fraud, whether it be dubious statistics and declarations by institutions, the very widespread plagiarism in education, the dependence on phony official handouts in journalism, or fake aesthetic gestures. This results less from malicious motives than from the personal need to impersonally fill the communications channels with something, be it PR releases, purchased term papers, ersatz news or pseudo-art. Officials, students, reporters and artists unable to meet the massive demands of communications systems, few of which shut down when no one has anything to say, become ingenuous frauds.

Institutions and learning also respond with overload-display, such as endless unconsumable committee reports, or, say, the current style in biographies of literary and political figures, which swell to absurd proportions in a mania for trivial detailing. Relentless collection and reproduction of information conjoins with a decline in coherence, and becomes its substitute. The means of communication become self-demanding and saturation the major end. Nor do the "higher arts" show much more immunity than the lowered arts from the saturation of technique-induced and media-faddish disposable styles. The presses will roll, the programming will go on, the institutions will demand, and they will all be filled and re-filled. Our communications, too, abhor a vacuum, except perhaps that of the self which they encourage within us.

Non-technical selectivity, that of sense and feeling, seems inappropriate. The libraries of the universities and the paper and film depositories of the corporations and the state become unstylishly monumental, as do our other garbage dumps. In spite of various elaborate systems for miniaturizing, digesting, compacting and indexing, we cannot achieve adequate ways to refine and dispose of our communications refuse. As with FBI and credit files, much of the accumulated information remains "raw" and open to misuse. As with book publishing, ritual confirmation of role becomes a major function, authorship certifying academics and other bureaucratic specialists, artistic pretenders and other status aggrandizers. As with book reviewing, selection and judging come out quite sycophantic, incompetent and arbitrary. Publishing and broadcasting are about as intellectual and honest as real estate brokerage.

Often the stock answers to the "communications problem" are to increase the problem itself. Many "liberal" critics of mass media news insist that we need more "news coverage," or even one or more new nation-wide systems of news broadcasting. Institutional reformers cry out for more committee studies and reports and public relations stuff. And sincere specialists everywhere self-interestedly demand more learned compilations and conference excretions and new subfields of research and grants and ego-reinforcing "communication." These pervasive responses must be part of a larger pathology. Just as our answer to nuclear war dangers has been to elaborate, produce and stockpile yet more nuclear weapons, so our answer to communications-information problems is to elaborate, produce and stockpile more of the same. Whether this logic inheres in technocratic order, or more deeply in the cast of mind and society which encourages that exponential processing, we see their fusion in a technocommunications religiosity.

Otherwise put, our poisoning by overdoses of incoherent information-communication is to be cured by homeopathically taking more of the same poison. Such magical treatment of sated sensibility runs through most futurist discussions of communications. "The knowledge factory of the future," the electronic mystics tell us, will be "a total information environment." By any available evidence and reasoning, mis-use, fraud, incoherence, satiation and ritual-control will also be massive characteristics of any further maximized communications systems.

Some futurists tell us that there will soon be a wonderful enlargement of television and its informing public services, with the current urban American access to about six channels to become, by way of cable TV, access to twenty to forty channels. By some weird extrapolation, multiplication of the same translates into diversity and freedom, and even increased art and enlightenment. The epitomization of this may be the McLuhanism of a few years ago in which by multiplying all the automobile models times all the optional accessories we arrive at the fantastic consumer options of 25 million transportation possibilities. Since the choices did not include significantly different power plants, or an inexpensively safe and well-crafted car, or comfortable and efficient public transportation, the millions of trivial variations merely confirmed the lack of significant choice which they helped to disguise. Parallel camouflaged standardization pervades publishing and broadcasting though because, unlike automobiles, communications are not subject to minimums of internal combustion and gravity, their variety may be even less real. There could of course be a small increase in mass media options for purposes of more sophisticated market exploitation and institutional control. In the mass media, in the developing home entertainment-information appliances, and in yet more unusual modes of further ritualizing play and thought, there may well be efforts to maximize special group appeals and profits rather than focusing on "One Maximum Audience." But given our social structure, any real increase in diversity and quality may only be slight. Radio stations devoted only to classical or rock music, magazines devoted only to popularized psychology or *au courant* art, may provide greater pleasures to their aficionados because of less distraction—a crucial longing of current overburdened audiences—and because of a distinctive vulgarization which highlights the identity of the special audience, thus giving further ritual appearance of personal definition and value. But the competitive conditioning of a still large and alienated audience promises no great increase in diversity or quality. More may usually be less when maximizing the inadequate for exploitative purposes. Put another way, the progress of technocommunications tends to be functional only, not intellectual or moral or aesthetic: ninety-nine ways of reproducing, redividing, redistributing the same material but not nine new ways of sensing, feeling and understanding the realities. Since our technocommunications have so far initiated little of significant aesthetic and intellectual quality, there is little reason to believe they ever will unless subject not to their own development but to radical changes in their social and cultural base.

Much of our current communications already produces excess, variously described as "the heavy communications overlay," "the information overload," "media saturation," "the knowledge explosion," "electronic enervation," "media shock," "stimuli redundancy," "technological burdening," or, in the superficially inflated metaphor of Alvin Toffler, "future shock." Some of the basic overload theories now current seem to derive from our knowledge of the effects of "sensory deprivation." The restricted laboratory animal or solitary invalid or prisoner suffers from a lack of stimuli and his symptoms of shock, anomie and apathy point to a physical as well as social and psychic decline. Over-population, over-stimulation and over-communication produce strikingly similar effects to deprivation. Too much, like too little, leads to withering and withdrawal at all levels. I emphasize the obvious: a "total information environment" or any other massive technocommunications system lacks human proportions. If not subject to the converging limitations of audience control, sensitively humane limits, and effective criticism, the communications will tend to impose their own processes and powers, violating the human sensibility historically oriented in previous communications. Part of this will be the impositions of the controllers of the communications, part will simply be the self-aggrandizing communications systems. Patently, the arbitrary and exploitative controls by our present bureaucratic-corporate marketplace do not, and cannot, provide sufficient limitation, criticism and participation. Technocommunications systems tend to take off on their own, over-riding and overloading the audiences, partly because a humanly reduced and passive sensibility well fits the demands of a technocracy and its controllers.

In a complex order, withdrawal from a communications and information overload takes various and even perverse ways. Communications addiction appears to be a major current way of inadequate or exasperated response. Desensitized or otherwise disoriented from the overload, the sated TV watcher, the obsessional memo-writer, the sports glutton, the fanatic info-accumulator, the telephone-head, or other communications compulsive may increase the dosage in desperate hope that more stimuli will overcome the deadening from overload. But this can only succeed in the sense that the traditional drunkard's hair-of-the-dog-that-bit-him provides momentary recuperation.

Yet total withdrawal from communications intoxication does not seem a generally viable possibility. Furthermore, as Emile Durkheim correctly predicted, mass industrial society reaches a condition in which "collective sentiments are weakened." As a result of the widespread feelings of isolation and uncertainty, substitute relationships and identifications, such as those provided by the mass media and other communications networks, become necessary. American society has completed a generation in which both the mass media drastically expanded and class education became

mass education. But, as many studies indicate, the increase in education has not made major differences in media intellectual and
aesthetic quality. The educated participate pretty much like everyone else in the ritual processing. I suggest they do so because there
is no other church in town.

From media content, one suspects that a generation of development and education produced a slight increase in sophistication. From audience responses, one suspects that affluence-educa-
tion produced a slight increase in resistance within the addictive
processing, by way of cynicism about the information, contempt for
aesthetic pretensions, and a defensively low-level of attention. Even
to these hardly radical responses, the media counter with increased
redundancy and ritualization, in an endless cycling of low-level
dissatisfaction. So we achieve, for the media and more generally,
the apathy called "tolerance" where anything goes, which means
nothing goes with high verve or great intensity. A certain madness
becomes normative, such as that of obscenely trumpeted pseudo-
products, a decade-long televised brutal war, increased alienation
from craft and intelligence, and much else. Dysfunction, in human
terms, becomes functional in a disintegrating culture held together
by shoddy but energetic technological systems.

Though compensatorily resisted, our communications overload must lead to exacerbation of the problems of society and sensibility. For instance, the administrative personality alienated from
those he manipulates must maximize his "in-puts," such as multiplying his directives, though memos memorialize only the unmemo-
rable and call forth a low level of response. Similarly with the "sensitivity sessions," new "internal information systems," and other
social scientized, psychologized and technologized substitutes for
common sentiments and authentic communications. Quite possibly,
of course, true rather than ritualized communications would break
up the bureaucracy since its authorities and products and purposes
may be illegitimate and unjustifiable. But *pretenses* at communication will not re-legitimatize authorities and purposes, or liberate
other vitalities. The radical problems remain under the ritual
camouflage of communications and information systems. New techniques and technologies get pressed into play to answer the now
self-evolving "communications problem," and the synthetic answer
becomes the real difficulty. As with new superhighways to relieve

the overload of old superhighways, which were to relieve the overload of highways, which were to relieve the overload of roads and streets, the labyrinth may become an infinite regress. This is technocracy.

The condition can be seen as dubious long before the labyrinth of technocommunications. The sages, such as Thoreau and Chuang-Tzu, objected to too many communications partly because wisdom requires intellectual open spaces, a recuperative wilderness of immediacy and contemplation. But when we everywhere find communications pollution some essentials have been lost, including crucial kinds of attention (not the mere inattention so necessary to survive our communications), solitude (not the mere loneliness of urban paranoia), and tangible communion (not mere media images and identities). For sensibility deprived of its crucial resources and burdened with synthetic substitutes must suffer disorientation. Art in this context starts out systematically strained and submerged. Desperate to attract attention to itself amidst the communications pollution, the techniques of art will be over-charged, the forms over-strained, the styles over-loaded. Hard rock music became so loud that it literally deafened its players and listeners. Popular melodramas, such as the "western" and detective and spy fables, became fantastically decadent with heroes as weird cripples and psychopaths. The reversed eros and violence become extreme and gratuitous. In such mannerism, the props take over the action and moral implications become comically perverse. As with conducting a conversation next to a turbine at a constant half-shout, attention must be lost because of inability at nuance and persuasive variation and proportion. Such exacerbated artistry becomes self-defeating, and probably must self-destruct.

A "double-bind" aesthetic takes over. Physical violation fuses with moral blandness, and tends to be perceived as the same. Ornate hysteria becomes one with simplex palliatives. We simultaneously get pushed towards passionate responses and pulled back into passive packaging. Intense demands for our concern conjoin with massive indifferentism. Probing the states of mass art forces upon us paradoxical descriptions of technological sensibility and its violent apathy, its optimistic despair, and its most insistent condition of overloaded emptiness. The stage directions for the personae in a technocracy may repeat the paralytic circle that concludes both

acts of *Waiting for Godot:* " 'Yes, let's go.' *They do not move.*"
Probably we should resist the simple conclusion that our "communications explosion" serves as cause rather than also as an effect of the failure of real communication. Surely our technology provides what we need to carry out some deeper imperatives of our culture and society. The Protestant Work Ethic secularized into productions for production's sake, and our technocommunications come out of it. The bureaucratic rationalization of an over-enlarged and over-powered America required massive ritualization through the media. The circuits must proliferate, and in a style which makes the proliferation of circuits our ultimate purpose. I also suspect that our exaltation of technocommunications systems—hardly anyone else seems to be seriously against them—expresses a desperate religious surrogate, a sensate mirage substituting for a good society.

Certainly our technocommunications developed from and still serve institutional advantages and ideological dominations, but the processing, I have argued, tends to take off on its own. Not all effects seem bad; demagoguery, contrary to our earlier prophets of mass communications dangers, may have declined, along with other impassioned responses. Some commentators relate the undeniable loss of legitimacy of institutional hierarchies to the bypassing of them by the communications systems. No doubt there are other advantages to the sensibility disoriented by endless media distractions. True, technocommunications can also serve oppositions, on limited occasions, carrying rebellious messages. But most such must be small and bitter fruit, pulped into the ritualized overload and synthetic sensibility which itself becomes the ultimate mode of control.

At some point, perhaps only recognizable in future perspective, the processing with technocommunications becomes sufficiently self-generating and self-serving so that freedom of communication doesn't even belong to those who own the communications. We may come under rule by our technology in the same sense that earlier cultures have been ruled by that which they worshipped. Of course technocracy is far from being, so far as we can see, complete, uniform, self-sufficient. Internal Luddditism and other ways of resistance continue, as do parts of traditional culture and counter-culture, and may limit the communications mania. Possibly the pervasive boredom and disorientation will create a resentful rage leading to apocalyptic tidings as the last message on the "news." Or the ritual processing and short-circuited sensibilities may merely decline into a full anemia of passion and purpose. Hence we may conclude with the rule of the sages: Too much of communications may finally be no communication at all. Perhaps we should add the Don Juan corollary: Just as the more one seduces the less one loves, so the more one is "informed" the less one knows. The seductions of maximized technocommunications and all their processing ways have become a religiosity which must be broken through. Otherwise the deadened sensibility and social catatonia of a technocracy may be the final news of the communications explosion.

the
cybernetic
consciousness

Science was born when philosophers deemphasized the conception of the nature of the universe in order to speculate and investigate "how" the universe behaved. To know "how," the scientist was eventually required to observe, test, hypothesize, and experiment. For the past two hundred years, perhaps longer, scientists have taken the study of the "how" to what some consider a dubious extreme. The degree of specialization today is a result of the view that depth tells us more than scope. Thus, within the macrocosmic endeavor of science, individuals have been increasingly encouraged to become microcosmic in their work.

Though Buckminster Fuller and Marshall McLuhan, among others, have called for "comprehensivist" or "generalist" students of the world, still more persuasively has the logic of science itself led us back to the "conception of the universe." The particular evolutionary development within science that brings us to a philosophic overview is cybernetics.

Throughout the history of science, individuals have made great discoveries about the universe itself which have had a great impact because of their implications for mankind. Though less appreciated in their own time, many scientific ideas have evolved into still greater social or cultural systems of thought. Newton created a powerful physics in his time, but his lasting contribution to human history is his world view: the idea of enlightenment, and all of the cultural effects stimulated by his vision of the world as mechanistic order.

When Newton entitled his first book "Optics," not only did he wish to describe the universal behavior of light, but he wanted also to reinforce the assumptions of "enlightenment," the idea that the universe was ordered, that this order was knowable, and that once perceived, it would allow men to live more compatibly with natural law, and thereby achieve harmony. This is merely one obvious example of the fact that science itself is encased by the culture that encourages it. The scientific endeavor is influenced by what it seeks to find and by what the society wishes to know.

Science is encapsulated by society, and their relationship is reciprocal. The direction of science will be influenced by the social support it receives and by the assumptions the scientists themselves make, and society will be changed by the scientists' reconceptions of the nature of the universe. It is more than an irony that in the birth throes of the twentieth century, Einstein conceived his theory of relativity, a phrase that has little competition as the major characteristic of this century.

The relationship between society and science has tended to remain an unspoken truth, at least within the discipline of science itself. Now, with the evolution of cybernetics, this process has been scientifically articulated.

Cybernetics is a system of thought resulting from the investigation of information processes. Out of the efforts of some to understand the behavior of data-processing machines and computers, and from such narrow concerns as, for example, how much information can be accurately transmitted through a wire, a comprehensive overview has emerged which not only tells us about parts of the whole, but also shows us the whole itself. Some call this "systems thinking," but I would prefer to describe it as today's version of the historically repetitive attempt to integrate human knowledge with a holistic view of the universe. Cybernetics can be thought of as the rehumanizing of scientific information; a generalization of all data into a metaphysical model.

I have called cybernetics holistic, and it is. Its implications and insights are available to the research scientist, the communications specialist, the sociologist, the psychologist, the cultural historian, and the poet. It is a sophisticated system of thought that could not have arisen had it not been for the cultural influences of existentialism and relativity theory. One might even argue that cybernetics is existentialist science, for it enables us to describe the entire workings of a system without recourse to first causes, the workings of the divine, or to cosmological order. In other words, it is a comprehensive model that does not necessarily have to refute the principles of relativity. It is a view of meaning that does not require the universe to be meaningful.

That cybernetics comes to us at the latter part of the twentieth century could not be more timely. If there was ever an era that needed some comprehensive overview of the diversity of experience and the endless purview of information, it is the present.

The ways cybernetics came to be derived are easy to retrace. When dealing with the behavior of machines, one encounters the problem of machine-human and machine-machine communication. Obviously, a machine will be of value only if we can communicate with it and tell it what we wish it to do. Usually this communication occurs within the design of the machine itself. However, with computers, we have designed machines that are capable of many tasks, and it is our job to instruct the machine for each specific one. As well as humans communicating desired tasks to machines, it is also necessary for the machine to indicate to humans when it does not have sufficient information to complete the task, or when it simply does not understand what is required of it. Thus, there must be some kind of language to expedite human-machine cooperation. As men came to study this question and to explore this language, they arrived at some very important insights into the nature of communication itself. The specific processes will be described in the essays that follow.

It was soon recognized that the theory of communication, its epistemological insights, its definition and understanding of message, feedback, voice and input-output processes—all occurring within relative and variable rates of change—tell us a great deal about our world if we consider man a machine and human environments as systems. The information generated by a study of human-machine and machine-machine communication became generalized into a broad field of study describing all communication processes.

If man can be metaphorically considered a machine, he can be redefined as an electro-chemical information system capable of various levels of multiple feedback. As the reader will see, this leads to holographic theories of the brain, psychic research, developments in neurobiology, studies of nonverbal communication, and a host of other related phenomena. If the human environment is considered as a system, a cybernetic investigation yields the connective-communicative aspects of the whole without expending energies in countless journeys into the parts.

Because new media are new communication systems, they will increase our cybernetic understanding and be better understood by a cybernetic analysis. The relationship is synergetic. The difficult cybernetics chapter appears first because an awareness of cybernetics is a necessary prelude to any further investigation of the media themselves. The parts should be discussed within the context of the whole. It is also necessary to consider John Lilly's clear articulation of the relationship between communication and mental health. Though some of the readings may be technical, the importance of their insights cannot be overestimated.

Chapter 3

mental health
and communication

John Lilly

Communication, when it succeeds, is one of man's greatest assets, and when it fails is his worst enemy. Each of us tries and succeeds to a certain extent to communicate with others in his immediate surroundings every day, hours at a time. As we vary as individuals so we vary in our talents in communication with one another. Some persons are expert communicators; each of us recognizes the experts. Yet an expert is not a scientist, is not a psychologist, nor any specialist necessarily. Such an expert communicator can be anyone. How does such a person become an expert in communication? Basically this is a question of mental health. The best communicators are those who are the most mentally healthy, happy, natural, spontaneous, disciplined persons.

Among the human species are persons who have severe difficulties in communication with other human beings. During our growth from infancy each of us has had difficulties which grade all the way from those of the child who yet had no language for communication, through the various human achievement levels: grade school, high school, college, job, profession. As we become older our skills at communication tend to increase, with experience and with practice and with study. For each one of us this is the most important study that we have ever undertaken: how to communicate with our fellow man is a constant and recurring problem of consuming interest.

"Mental Health and Communication." From *The Mind of the Dolphin*, by John Lilly. Copyright © 1967 by John C. Lilly. Reprinted by permission of Doubleday & Company, Inc. and The Harold Matson Company, Inc.

We want understanding, love, and respect; we receive them through communicating what is in our minds. We want to give understanding, love, and respect; we can give only through communication and only to those who can communicate in turn.

Our mental health is measured by how well we communicate with our fellow men and women. As Freud emphasized, the special communication called sexual activities gives one a rule of thumb of the success that a person has as a healthy human being. If one has exhilarating, stimulating, and fulfilling sexual experiences in the heterosexual sphere, he is mentally healthy. If one's work is successful, expanding, and happy, he is mentally healthy. In these two spheres (in the love life and in the work life) of a given individual are the major clues to a person's success as an individual. This is the outside view of one's personal accomplishments and personal behaviors.

However, the inside view (the almost secret view) of one's self that he protects from the outside society says similar things. If one, as it were, deep within his adult self knows that his sexual activities are satisfying, guilt-free, and give intense pleasure to his partner, he has a deep happiness on which he bases the rest of his life.

If one's work presents novelty, variety, and a sense of internal and external progress as judged by himself (and eventually by the others outside himself), he then adds to the happiness of his love life by the accomplishments in the external world.

Thus our problem in our own species is achieving a basic communication with our fellow men and fellow women, so deep that each of us and each of them can be satisfied in very basic ways. If our communication is blocked, the satisfactory performance of our love life and our work life is blocked. If we have an unconscious and a conscious desire to communicate with our fellow men we can succeed. However, we must know ourselves in order to communicate. We must know the kind of things that we project into other people "as if" they are communicating them to us but are really not so doing.

This phenomena of projection of ourselves (our thoughts and our expectations) into others is a very human problem. We miss our goals by assuming that others are what we want them to be or that they are saying or communicating by other means what we want them to communicate. This problem of projection blocks a large fraction of true communication. How do we do this wishful, false realizing?

Our relatively large minds (brains) act as computers that can make models inside themselves of other human minds and their activities. Each of us knows that we construct models of other persons: one has a model of his wife in his head; she in turn has a model of her husband in hers. Each of us has a model of each child as it comes along; the models must grow with the child or there is communication trouble. The model of the wife must change in the husband as the wife changes and grows; the model of the husband in the wife must change as the real person changes. Otherwise there is a severe breakdown of communication.

One must change the models of one's parents and not project them into the model of one's wife or husband or children. The modeling that we did as children (of the adults in our surroundings) has the primitive features on which all the others eventually are built. However, unless built as growing, changing models, the childish models can be defective, can be incomplete, and eventually can be shown to be what they really are, "childish models," needing change and growth. Mentally healthy persons start with growing, changing models and see to it that growth continues.

Thus projection involves the use of inappropriate intransigent models of other human beings. If one has a realistic model of one's wife or husband (the model that corresponds more or less with the reality of that person), he or she then successfully communicates with the real person. He does not ask that particular real person to do impossible or contradictory things to satisfy his fantasies; he asks appropriate, realizable things to satisfy him.

Similarly, if one knows his own basic deep needs, he can communicate in terms of ethics, morals, manners, instincts, the acquisition of new knowledge, the nurturing and teaching of children, the building and maintenance of his own home, the encouragement of his friends, the performance of his work, the participation in the national and international life of his species. If one can realize that he is a unique individual, unrepeated since the beginning of his species, and can also confer this honor on each other human individual, he can then spend the time to learn his own internal language, and the internal language of each other individual, learn how to translate each into the commonly shared language and thus succeed in communication.

The human species has found quite empirically that the best communication is by those who closely resemble one another and who are placed in long-term close contact with one another. Isolated communities develop and maintain singularities in the language used; they develop and maintain customs of dress, of ritual, of loving, and of working uniquely theirs. They can also develop what has been termed "fear of the stranger" or "xenophobia" in many instances. In other instances xenophobia fails to appear or somehow is worked through by the local community, and strangers are welcomed among them. The projection of one's fears outward onto the unknown or the unfamiliar, beyond one's own group, nation, or species, creates a dangerous communication paralysis.

In the modern world with the hydrogen bombs and threats of extinction, we must, finally, examine carefully our best means of communication with interpersonal man, of group to ever larger group. We must support research in these areas of communication. We must support research that shows promise of giving us new insight into interhuman communication. *For the mental health of each one of us, for the national and international peace of all of us, communication is a paramount and pressing issue.* We can no longer allow the "glass walls" that have risen between us (most dramatically in the mentally ill, and in the international cases) to exist, much less to influence our desires and our needs to communicate. This book demonstrates the relevance of the study of communication with the bottlenose dolphin to these extremely important future advances in human communication: through dolphins we will see ourselves as others see us. Through dolphin communication efforts we will help ourselves. . . .

The truly deep problems of the mentally ill are communication problems. A mentally ill person for some reason or another cannot and hence will not communicate adequately with other human beings. The reasons among the many unique ill individuals are myriad. The reasons are under intensive scrutiny in many areas of medical and mental health research.

Some of the genetic factors, the "inherited defects," are being turned up in the recent research on chromosomes in the human. For

example, several determinable physical signs of an altered inherit-
ance have been found in the chromosomal studies. Some forms of
mental illness depend upon such inherited, determinable defects.
These defects are manifested by sometimes obvious anatomical
changes in the appearance of the human being, sometimes in an
obvious biochemical change (with the excretion of the urine of
particular "abnormal" substances). Sometimes there are only peculiar behaviors, and, most relevant to our present discussion, only
peculiar kinds of communication of types not normally encountered.

This group of patients are those with built-in "errors" of in-
heritance. These are the genetically determined and clinically de-
tectable "errors." Such cases are relatively infrequent in occurrence.

Most of us who manage to survive all of the exigencies of conception, gestation, birth, and infancy are uniquely different, one
from another. The evidence for this uniqueness is manifold. If one
attempts to graft the skin of one person onto another person, the
second person develops immunities against that grafted skin, and
it eventually sloughs off. A careful examination of the mechanisms
underlying the development of these immunities shows that each of
us is so biochemically different that we reject the live tissues of
another. These biochemical differences may extend into almost all
aspects of our lives. Each of our neuronal patterns of activity is
unique (EEGs, etc.). Perhaps each of us is so uniquely different that
our thought processes, as well as our neuronal patterns of activity,
are uniquely different. However, there seems to be at least potentially enough commonality of thinking and feeling to achieve
communication and to maintain us as a species. We know that there
is enough commonality of anatomy, at least of gross anatomy, to
perpetuate the species. If there is not, that individual has no children. It is almost as if in the gross large picture we are forced by
survival contingencies to look alike. As the picture becomes more
and more microscopic, and we analyze closer and closer to the individual selves, the differences become obvious, inescapable, and de-
termining.

The "general purpose" nature of large parts of our brains is
the saving grace which allows one individual to communicate with
another. The uniqueness built into the biochemistry generates a
brain which in the patterns of activity and in microscopic and
molecular detail is unique. As over the thousands of generations in

evolution the number of neurons has increased to the thirteen billions that we have, a common power or property has developed in most human brains. The important common power is the ability of this brain to assume the tasks of making models of creatures and persons in its surrounds. This is the fundamental property which allows communication to take place.

We can develop and share a language among uniquely different individuals because each of those individuals can take on enough of the commonality of language within his own brain to allow communication. But we must never forget that the thinking processes of the individual are still uniquely his or hers. Only certain aspects are common and shared. We may have the illusion of penetrating completely into the mental life of another human being through language, but this is impossible. Each of us is so uniquely different and so uniquely himself that we cannot yet so penetrate. It is a delusion to presume that one can. Laziness fosters this belief.

Chapter 4

cybernetics
in history

Norbert Wiener

Since the end of World War II, I have been working on the many ramifications of the theory of messages. Besides the electrical engineering theory of the transmission of messages, there is a larger field which includes not only the study of language but the study of messages as a means of controlling machinery and society, the development of computing machines and other such automata, certain reflections upon psychology and the nervous system, and a tentative new theory of scientific method. This larger theory of messages is a probabilistic theory, an intrinsic part of the movement that owes its origin to Willard Gibbs. . . .

Until recently, there was no existing word for this complex of ideas, and in order to embrace the whole field by a single term, I felt constrained to invent one. Hence "Cybernetics," which I derived from the Greek word *kubernetes,* or "steersman," the same Greek word from which we eventually derive our word "governor." Incidentally, I found later that the word had already been used by Ampère with reference to political science, and had been introduced in another context by a Polish scientist, both uses dating from the earlier part of the nineteenth century.

I wrote a more or less technical book entitled *Cybernetics* which was published in 1948. In response to a certain demand for me to make its ideas acceptable to the lay public, I published the first edition of *The Human Use of Human Beings* in 1950. Since then the subject has grown from a few ideas shared by Drs. Claude Shannon, Warren Weaver, and myself, into an established region of research. . . .

In giving the definition of Cybernetics in the original book, I classed communication and control together. Why did I do this? When I communicate with another person, I impart a message to him, and when he communicates back with me he returns a related message which contains information primarily accessible to him and not to me. When I control the actions of another person, I communicate a message to him, and although this message is in the imperative mood, the technique of communication does not differ from that of a message of fact. Furthermore, if my control is to be effective I must take cognizance of any messages from him which may indicate that the order is understood and has been obeyed.

It is [my] thesis . . . that society can only be understood through a study of the messages and the communication facilities which belong to it; and that in the future development of these messages and communication facilities, messages between man and machines, between machines and man, and between machine and machine, are destined to play an ever-increasing part.

When I give an order to a machine, the situation is not essentially different from that which arises when I give an order to a person. In other words, as far as my consciousness goes I am aware of the order that has gone out and of the signal of compliance that has come back. To me, personally, the fact that the signal in its intermediate stages has gone through a machine rather than through a person is irrelevant and does not in any case greatly change my relation to the signal. Thus the theory of control in engineering, whether human or animal or mechanical, is a chapter in the theory of messages.

Naturally there are detailed differences in messages and in problems of control, not only between a living organism and a machine, but within each narrower class of beings. It is the purpose of Cybernetics to develop a language and technique that will enable us indeed to attack the problem of control and communication in general, but also to find the proper repertory of ideas and techniques to classify their particular manifestations under certain concepts.

The commands through which we exercise our control over our environment are a kind of information which we impart to it. Like any form of information, these commands are subject to disorganization in transit. They generally come through in less coherent fashion and certainly not more coherently than they were sent. In control and communication we are always fighting nature's tendency to degrade the organized and to destroy the meaningful; the tendency, as Gibbs has shown us, for entropy to increase.

. . . Man is immersed in a world which he perceives through his sense organs. Information that he receives is co-ordinated through his brain and nervous system until, after the proper process of storage, collation, and selection, it emerges through effector organs, generally his muscles. These in turn act on the external world, and also react on the central nervous system through receptor organs such as the end organs of kinaesthesia; and the information received by the kinaesthetic organs is combined with his already accumulated store of information to influence future action.

Information is a name for the content of what is exchanged with the outer world as we adjust to it, and make our adjustment felt upon it. The process of receiving and of using information is the process of our adjusting to the contingencies of the outer environment, and of our living effectively within that environment. The needs and the complexity of modern life make greater demands on this process of information than ever before, and our press, our museums, our scientific laboratories, our universities, our libraries and textbooks, are obliged to meet the needs of this process or fail in their purpose. To live effectively is to live with adequate information. Thus, communication and control belong to the essence of man's inner life, even as they belong to his life in society. . . .

The machine which acts on the external world by means of messages is . . . familiar. The automatic photoelectric door opener is known to every person who has passed through the Pennsylvania Station in New York, and is used in many other buildings as well. When a message consisting of the interception of a beam of light is sent to the apparatus, this message actuates the door, and opens it so that the passenger may go through.

The steps between the actuation of a machine of this type by sense organs and its performance of a task may be as simple as in the case of the electric door; or it may be in fact of any desired degree of complexity within the limits of our engineering techniques. A complex action is one in which the data introduced, which we call the *input*, to obtain an effect on the outer world, which we call the *output*, may involve a large number of combinations. These are combinations both of the data put in at the moment and of the records taken from the past stored data which we call the *memory*. These are recorded in the machine. The most complicated machines yet made which transform input data into output data are the high-speed electrical computing machines. . . . The determination of the mode of conduct of these machines is given through a special sort of input, which frequently consists of punched cards or tapes or of magnetized wires, and which determines the way in which the machine is going to act in one operation, as distinct from the way in which it might have acted in another. Because of the frequent use of punched or magnetic tape in the control, the data which are fed in, and which indicate the mode of operation of one of these machines for combining information, are called the *taping*.

. . . Man and the animal have a kinaesthetic sense, by which they keep a record of the position and tensions of their muscles. For any machine subject to a varied external environment to act effectively it is necessary that information concerning the results of its own action be furnished to it as part of the information on which it must continue to act. For example, if we are running an elevator, it is not enough to open the outside door because the orders we have given should make the elevator be at that door at the time we open it. It is important that the release for opening the door be dependent on the fact that the elevator is actually at the door; otherwise something might have detained it, and the passenger might step into the empty shaft. This control of a machine on the basis of its *actual* performance rather than its *expected* performance is known as *feedback,* and involves sensory members which are actuated by motor members and perform the function of *tell-tales* or *monitors*—that is, of elements which indicate a performance. It is the function of these mechanisms to control the mechanical tendency toward disorganization; in other words, to produce a temporary and local reversal of the normal direction of entropy. I have just mentioned the elevator as an example of feedback. There are other cases where the importance of feedback is even more apparent. For example, a gun-pointer takes information from his instruments of observation, and conveys it to the gun, so that the latter will point in such a direction that the missile will pass through the moving target at a certain time. Now, the gun itself must be used under all conditions of weather. In some of these the grease is warm, and the gun swings easily and rapidly. Under other conditions the grease is frozen or mixed with sand, and the gun is slow to answer the orders given to it. If these orders are reinforced by an extra push given when the gun fails to respond easily to the orders and lags behind them, then the error of the gunpointer will be decreased. To obtain a performance as uniform as possible, it is customary to put into the gun a control feedback element which reads the lag of the gun behind the position it should have according to the orders given it, and which uses this difference to give the gun an extra push.

It is true that precautions must be taken so that the push is not too hard, for if it is, the gun will swing past its proper position, and will have to be pulled back in a series of oscillations, which may well become wider and wider, and lead to a disastrous instability. If the feedback system is itself controlled—if, in other words, its own entropic tendencies are checked by still other controlling mechanisms—and kept within limits sufficiently stringent, this will not occur, and the existence of the feedback will increase the stability of performance of the gun. In other words, the performance will become less dependent on the frictional load; or what is the same thing, on the drag created by the stiffness of the grease.

Something very similar to this occurs in human action. If I pick up my cigar, I do not will to move any specific muscles. Indeed in many cases, I do not know what those muscles are. What I do is to turn into action a certain feedback mechanism; namely, a reflex in which the amount by which I have yet failed to pick up the cigar is turned into a new and increased order to the lagging muscles, whichever they may be. In this way, a fairly uniform voluntary command will enable the same task to be performed from widely varying initial positions, and irrespective of the decrease of contraction due to fatigue of the muscles. Similarly, when I drive a car, I do not follow out a series of commands dependent simply on a mental image of the road and the task I am doing. If I find the car swerving too much to the right, that causes me to pull it to the left. This depends on the actual performance of the car, and not simply on the road; and it allows me to drive with nearly equal efficiency a light Austin or a heavy truck, without having formed separate habits for the driving of the two. . . .

It is my thesis that the physical functioning of the living individual and the operation of some of the newer communication machines are precisely parallel in their analogous attempts to control entropy through feedback. Both of them have sensory receptors as one stage in their cycle of operation: that is, in both of them there exists a special apparatus for collecting information from the outer world at low energy levels, and for making it available in the operation of the individual or of the machine. In both cases these external messages are not taken *neat*, but through the internal transforming powers of the apparatus, whether it be alive or dead. The information is then turned into a new form available for the further stages of performance. In both the animal and the machine this performance is made to be effective on the outer world. In both of them, their *performed* action on the outer world, and not merely their *intended* action, is reported back to the central regulatory apparatus. This complex of behavior is ignored by the average man, and in particular does not play the role that it should in our habitual analysis of society; for just as individual physical responses may be seen from this point of view, so may the organic responses of society itself. I do not mean that the sociologist is unaware of the existence and complex nature of communications in society, but until recently he has tended to overlook the extent to which they are the cement which binds its fabric together.

We have seen in this [discussion] the fundamental unity of a complex of ideas which until recently had not been sufficiently associated with one another, namely, the contingent view of physics that Gibbs introduced as a modification of the traditional, Newtonian conventions, the Augustinian attitude toward order and conduct which is demanded by this view, and the theory of the message among men, machines, and in society as a sequence of events in time which, though it itself has a certain contingency, strives to hold back nature's tendency toward disorder by adjusting its parts to various purposive ends.

Chapter 5

language and
communication

Jagjit Singh

Although cybernetics has now become a miscellany of loosely related activities, we shall use the term here to denote an interdisciplinary inquiry into the nature and physical basis of human intelligence, with the object of reproducing it synthetically. Since human intelligence shows itself in the complexity of man's total conduct, such an introspective probe must naturally begin with the construction of mechanisms that will exhibit comparable complexity of behavior. But to construct the latter we must somehow specify in language the complexity we wish to embody in the machine. Consequently, the complexity of the system we attempt to define will inevitably be limited by our power of processing the information communicated in the language we use. Unfortunately, our information-absorbing powers, when we employ the language of our daily discourse, are notoriously limited. The only way of overcoming this handicap is to make machines that understand languages—machine codes—with far greater capacity to gobble and digest coded information fed into them than our own. . . . Several machine languages or codes of sufficient sophistication have recently been devised to permit description of highly complicated systems. There is thus a close but reciprocal tie-up between the complexity of a system and the language used to specify complexity for communicating it to the processing machine. Language and communication on

"Language and Communication." From *Great Ideas in Information Theory, Language, and Cybernetics,* by Jagjit Singh (New York: Dover Publications, Inc., 1966). Reprinted by permission of the publisher.

the one hand and complexity of artificial intelligent systems on the other are, therefore, closely related. Advances in one—say, the power of language—enable the specification of more complex systems; whereas the construction of more complex systems that such specification allows leads to the invention of more powerful languages or machine codes. Thanks to parallel advances in machine codes and in the design of machines able to manipulate the information they embody, it has recently been possible to devise highly complex communication machines and control systems capable of imitating human behavior to some extent. Such, for example, are the machines which communicate with one another by means of a code or language very much as human beings do. There are others which store data put into them and thus exhibit what we call memory. This process has been extended to confer on these machines even the power to learn, although the technique of building and employing such machines . . . is still very rudimentary and imperfect. However, despite their imperfections, the study of all these kinds of machines has inevitably led to a new understanding of the mechanism of language, communication, memory, and learning in human beings.

The new understanding fostered by cybernetics is not only leading to the creation of improved technical devices (enabling a computer or even a summit leader to speak to its/his counterpart across the continent at the flick of a few switches) but is providing a basis for the design of what Hans Freudenthal calls "Lincos," a new language for cosmic intercourse. Beginning with a Lincos broadcast of such universal truths as "twice two makes four," it may be possible to develop sufficient vocabulary to converse even on God, love, Universal Mind and the like with celestial beings in other planetary worlds of the Milky Way and beyond.

The ability of cybernetics to take in its stride such a wide diversity of activities as the design of robots to guide satellites in their courses, pursue missiles, run refineries, or monitor telephone exchanges, on the one hand, and that of ersatz brains, intelligence amplifiers, and Lincos, on the other, stems from a basic unity pervading both types of control and communication mechanisms—the naturally occurring type found in animals as well as the artificially contrived one in manmade automata. It shows itself most strikingly in the rudimentary imitations of life embodied in the remarkable toys of electrophysiologists like Ross Ashby and Grey Walter. Ashby's creature, appropriately christened *machina spora,* for example, behaves as a "fireside cat or dog which only stirs when disturbed, and then methodically finds a comfortable position and goes to sleep again." [1] Actually it is merely a rig of electronic circuits similar to the reflex arcs within the spinal cord of an animal. Grey Walter's wandering tortoise, *machina speculatrix,* on the other hand,

> is never still except when "feeding"—that is, when the batteries are being recharged. Like the restless creatures in a drop of pond water it bustles around in a series of swooping curves so that in an hour it will investigate several hundred square feet of ground. In its exploration of any ordinary room it inevitably encounters many obstacles; but apart from stairs and rugs, there are few situations from which it cannot extricate itself. [2]

What the Ashby-Walter pieces of complicated electrical circuitry attempt to do is to simulate the mental activity of the brain, that is, its thinking process, in a rudimentary manner by substituting wire in place of nerve fiber, hardware in place of flesh, and electromagnetic wave in place of the mysterious pulse in the living nerve fiber. Although the purposive lifelike behavior of such simulacra and other servo systems devised for the automatic control of machinery and plant by no means warrants the assumption that the animal nervous systems function in the same way, their study is nevertheless an essential preliminary to our understanding of animal brains as well as of human behavior patterns such as speech and other habits. This is why cybernetics is now a confluence of many streams of knowledge—neurophysiology, biochemistry, computers, information theory, automation, mathematical logic, probability, linguistics, and psychology, to name only a few. This is also why it is likely to have even more momentous consequences for the future of mankind than the discovery of atomic energy, unless we happen to abuse the latter by blowing ourselves up in a fit of suicidal stupidity.

Indeed, cybernetics has already sparked what has been aptly called the *second* industrial revolution. In the first industrial revolu-

---

[1] *The Living Brain,* by W. Grey Walter, Penguin Books, Inc., 1961, p. 111.
[2] *Ibid.,* p. 114.

tion first steam-driven machines and then the internal combustion engine took over the physical work that man or his beasts of burden used to do. But man still had to perform all important control functions to guide the engines he set to work. In the second industrial revolution even such guidance has now begun to devolve in increasing measure on other machines. If the first revolution was the outcome of the efforts of a long succession of *application-oriented* engineers like Porta, Newcomen, Watt, and Boulton, the second sprouted from the labors of pure mathematicians like Leibnitz, Pascal, Babbage, and Boole. Charles Babbage made elaborate blueprints of automatic computers, showing a perspicacity and vision not unlike Leonardo's in foreseeing the day of airplanes. Both were far ahead of the technology of their times. Whereas the realization of Leonardo's dream had to wait for the invention of the internal combustion engine, that of Babbage had to wait for the emergence of electronics with its gift of electronic relays, vacuum tubes, magnetic tapes, and transistors. Once the new electronic tools to implement Babbage's ideas came to hand, it did not take long to automatize computation. Surprising as it may seem, automatization of computation immediately paved the way for automatizing industrial operations. The movement began with the chemical industry and soon spread to the telephone system and automobile production during the 1920's. It now bids fair to encompass all the remaining areas.

The reason electronics was able to advance automation so speedily is that for many years it was devoted almost entirely to the communication or transmission of information from one place to another. Besides wire and radio communication, it included sound recording, hearing aids, television, and other information-handling systems. In each of these applications the principal objective of the various pieces of equipment is to reproduce the input signal with as high fidelity as possible at the output device. From mere hi-fi transmission of information to its "processing" is but a step. Nevertheless, it was a major advance in that the electronic relays, vacuum tubes, transistors, and other similar control and communication devices which facilitate the processing of information are to the power machines they control what brain is to brawn. The control systems operate with low expenditure of energy and their mechanical efficiency is of no consequence, because their basic function is not to transform energy but to *process* information. The inputs of such systems are often the electronic counterparts of such animal sense organs as eyes and ears—thermostats, photoelectric cells, microphones, or stain gauges. The outputs are the analogues of an animal's muscles or communicating organs—loudspeakers, electric typewriters, and electric motors. Internally, the information being processed takes the form of the passage of electrical signals from one part of the system to another. It therefore follows that the functioning of the control devices depends primarily on proper flow or processing of information communicated by one part of the automatized system to another.

Control and communications systems attempt to do this in one of two ways or both. *Either* they merely transmit information with the least possible distortion, as in teletype, telephony, radio, and television, or they "process" the flow of such information from one part to another of an integrated whole in order to carry through a closely knit sequence of operations, whether industrial or computational, without human intervention at any intermediate stage. What then is this "information" with whose "flow" and "processing" the science of cybernetics and communication engineering are chiefly concerned?

In ordinary speech we use the word "information" as a synonym for news, knowledge, intelligence, report, and so on. It is an amalgam of so many vague and imprecise meanings that a scientist has to purify from the blend of its diverse connotations the one he requires for his purpose, very much as a chemist purifies a substance in order to study its behavior. In the communication engineer's purification of the term the stress is on the quantitative aspect of the *flow* in a *network* of an *intangible* attribute called *information*. It is measured (in a manner to be defined more precisely later) by its "news" value, that is, the extent of surprise it causes to the recipient. To understand the rationale underlying the surprise-value theory of information measure, consider a typical communications network. No matter whether it is a network of telegraph and telephone lines or of radio and television channels or even a mere living-room conversation, any such network will consist of at least three main parts:

(i) Transmitter or source.

(ii) Receiver.

(iii) Channel which conveys the communiqué from the transmitter to the receiver.

For example, in the case of a living-room conversation, the speaker is the source or transmitter, the air which carries his voice is the channel, and the listener is the receiver. Practical cases are generally much more elaborate, consisting of a number of sources and receivers in a complex network. The problems of transmission of information in such complex networks are somewhat analogous to those of electric transmission in a power grid using several inter-connected generating stations to supply a number of towns. In both cases one seeks optimal schemes of distribution of the commodity flowing in the network on the basis of an appropriate criterion of efficiency of transmission. When the communiqué is tangible and therefore readily measurable, as in the case of an electric grid or a manufacturing belt, the problems encountered in the study of the communications system are of the types somewhat familiar to engineers and operational analysts. Such, for instance, is the case with an electric power network, where the criterion of efficiency is obviously the minimization of the heat loss *during* transmission. One way of accomplishing this (apart from using low-resistance transmission wires) is to increase the voltage at the input terminals of the line by installing a step-up voltage transformer and reducing the voltage to the prescribed level at the output terminals by another step-down transformer.

When, however, the flow in the network is an intangible like "information," as in the problem of the communications engineer concerned with sending messages by telegraph, telephone, radio, or otherwise, the criterion of efficiency naturally is the transmission of messages with minimum distortion at maximum speed and minimum cost. It happens that just as we may use a transformer to improve the efficiency of an electrical transmission system so also we may use what is called an encoder to improve the efficiency of a communication channel. The reason is that an encoded message is less liable to distortion by channel noise. Any communications system then may be symbolically represented as follows:

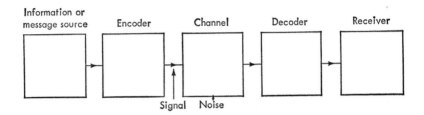

The information or message source selects a desired message out of a set of possible messages, just as a telegraphist selects one from a tray of messages awaiting transmission. The selected message may consist of written or spoken words or of pictures, music, and the like. The encoder codes the message or transforms it into the signal, which is actually sent over the communication channel from the encoder to the decoder. In the case of telephony, the channel is a wire, which carries the signal, a varying electrical current, produced by the encoder or the apparatus that transforms the sound pressure of source voice into the varying electrical current. In telegraphy the encoder codes the written words of the message into sequences of interrupted currents of varying lengths (dots, dashes, and spaces). In oral speech the information source is the brain, the encoder the voice mechanism that produces the varying sound pressure (the signal) which is transmitted through the air, the channel. In radio the channel is simply space and the signal the transmitted electromagnetic wave. Likewise, at the receiver's terminal a decoder is employed to transform the encoded message into the original form acceptable to the receiver. In other words, while the encoder transforms the intangible input commodity called "information" into a new form, the decoder performs the reverse operation to recover the encoded commodity in its pristine purity. In actual practice, however, there is no such pure recovery. One has always to contend with the vitiations of noise which in physical systems inevitably prevent perfect communication. These unwanted additions to the signal may be distortions of sound as in telephony, static as in radio, disfigurations in shape or shading of pictures as in television, or errors in transmission as in telegraphy. In all such communications systems the fundamental problem is to devise an appropriate measure of the "information" that they handle or process so as to use it to improve their "efficiency" in diverse ways such as enhancing the capacity of the channel to carry information to its optimal level and/or minimizing the adverse effects of noise vitiating its transmission.

Chapter 6

video tape
and the
communications revolution

Barry Schwartz

In a recent letter from the Editor-in-Chief of *Arts in Society,* Edward
L. Kamarck, I was asked to write an article of a broadly speculative
nature on the following:

- Possible insights for the arts coming out of the rapidly growing
  communications theory
- Futurist thinking and planning as they relate to the arts, arts development and culture
- The range of possibilities (and hazards) for the arts opened up by
  the new media, resources, materials and techniques
- The cultural problems, impacts and opportunities—both likely
  and already manifest—posed by the new technologies of communication
- The definition of a more responsible social role for communications in our culture and a contingent consideration of the necessary social changes.

Mr. Kamarck's letter communicates as much about print as through
it. At first, I was hesitant to quote from it; I may be violating a print
ethic. Print is a communication medium with implied degrees of
privacy. It is personal, and has a varying impact depending on how
it is used and with whom. Thus print supports hierarchies of in-

"Video Tape and the Communications Revolution" (revised), by Barry
Schwartz. Published originally as "The Communications Revolution: Lower
Rates for Long Distance Telephone Calls, or the Transformation of Society."
From *Arts in Society,* vol. 9, no. 2 (Summer–Fall 1972). Reprinted by permission
of the author and publisher.

formation as well as secrecy, fragmentation and concepts of communication propriety. Print begins in isolation and only reaches an audience of more than one by an expenditure of energy. The decoding of print requires that the reader too must exist in isolation. When he reads, he can do little more. He must stop experience in order to participate in a communication process.

These qualities do not characterize the new communications media. It is nearly impossible to communicate with the new media in privacy. The new media are electric; it takes energy to restrict the flow of information. The new media communicate publicly; there are no more secrets; no more private discussions.

Print is essentially a cognitive experience. Print encourages the invention of categories and then requires that they be legitimized. The history of theological writing is one excellent example of how much energy can be spent trying to validate print categories. Print is concerned largely with ideas and analysis. If I am to write this article on communications, I must *think about and analyze* the problems that have been posed. I must use cognitive units to give order by their meanings to a world that, if unordered, appears as frightening, chaotic and inexplicable. If I chose to use one of the new media—video, for example—I would comply with Mr. Kamarck's request by *doing,* not by thinking. My response would be an action through the media; I would respond rather than work out an appropriate response. It is one of the more revolutionary features of the new media that *communication is simultaneous with experience.* The communication process is not a reflection of experience but a part of it. Thus, the outstanding feature of new media is their capacity to provide feedback. If the new media are to affect the arts, it will be in the direction of leading artistic experience back into real time, not delayed-response time; the artist will be encouraged to unify life experience and artistic experience into the same space in real time. Artists will become highly sophisticated forms of human feedback in real-time situations.

Today's world can not be ordered effectively by print or by the still-frame aesthetic of photography, painting and image making. The world is surrounded by an envelope of electronically communicated information. Print is encapsulated by the electronic environment. Print may in fact confuse us because it leads us to the erroneous assumption that our description of an experience resembles the experience, that the phrasing of a problem is a perimeter containing the problem. Print, however, does poorly as a container for contemporary experience. What is needed is the dynamic frame of the newer communications media.

Print allows no feedback. If Mr. Kamarck and I were able to communicate telepathically we could discuss his letter and my response to it before he would sit down to write me. The letter itself would be merely a record of what was communicated, not a medium through which we communicate. The new media are not telepathic (not yet), but insofar as they do permit the process I have described, we may think of the new media as slow-motion telepathy. By slow motion, I may mean only microseconds from coded communication to decoded message to feedback. Like telepathy, the new media are electric.

Each moment we are inundated with electric information via television, radio, teletype, record players, tape machines, computers and satellite communications. In this environment young people are first acculturated into the society electronically. All learn a visual-electronic literacy long before they learn print. A child who stutters when reading aloud may be indefatigable and fluent on the telephone. The inevitable outcome of exposure to the new media is that society is relinquishing the view that print has a more valuable function than reportage of sporting events or the instructions to the toaster. Despite the efforts of the print nostalgia cult called college, slowly but irreversibly the importance of print is subsiding.

For most people, print is after the fact. They are becoming accustomed to media that communicate in real time. Of course, real time, all the time, is very taxing. Survival may come to be more dependent on the durability of the nervous system than on the cognitive muscularity of the brain. Some analysts of the electronic environment (energy trippers) proclaim that modern man is a crude form of electric man, whose advanced nervous system presumably places him higher on the evolutionary track.

Electricity holds no allegiances to custom, national boundaries, geography, or roadblocks. An electric perception is *de facto* an ecological one. The launching of satellites and the pictures they electronically communicate constitute feedback to the earth that it is a planet. Countries, states, institutions are aggregates of matter;

they hold bodies. In the electric environment, we are told we are no longer convinced of the need for separation and fragmentation. Electricity brings us together. In the electric current, we find a holistic view of man in the world. We will seek communality rather than egoistic death-wish power drives.

In the electronic environment reality is only one's accumulated information. For twenty-five years, this country has created myths of China. Our great men of state have characterized her as "the yellow peril," and her people as "yellow dwarfs with pen knives." But in the electronic environment, there are no men of state; only men of media. The first few seconds of live video coverage via satellite of Nixon's visit to China destroyed twenty-five years of illusions for many people. All at once China was no more threatening than Dodge City or the Twilight Zone; no further away than our chief celebrity, the man usually televised from the White House, the only man in America who can preempt the regular programming at will.

According to a *Newsweek* poll, the average American household watches more than six hours of television a day. There are more television sets in homes than telephones, bathtubs or refrigerators. In 1948, 200,000 American homes had television, and there were fifteen broadcasting stations. Today, 95 percent of homes have television—14 million of them in color—and there are 520 broadcasting stations. In America in 1973, there are few things more *essential* than television.

Broadcast information is our environment. Unfortunately the use of the media is predicated on commercial-exploitative values rather than on cultural or educational ones. Recently advertising studios have begun to run programs which they have packaged to show between their commercials. These programs are primarily geared toward developing and advancing consumerism, toward creating a passive, anxiety-ridden populace, ever ready to buy the latest innovation on the American dream. Television, we are reminded, is a mass medium, and mass media cater to what those with broadcast power euphemistically call the "common denominator."

Now hold on to your antennas. This situation is about to be altered dramatically. Enter video. Broadcast television is a one-way communication directing an audience toward programming with which they have no relationship. Now with a hand-held camera, a playback-record deck and a monitor or an RF unit (which plays back through your regular TV set), you are able to create your own programming. You are your own commercials.

The ability to make your own "software" coincides with the maturation of the first generation to grow up electrically. This generation has watched television all its life. It is not surprising to find that as adults, they insist that there be a new television, one that is relevant to the lives of the viewers, not to the profits of the broadcasters. This generation is committed to the box, the video medium, and watching television. It was inevitable that they would demand and utilize a technology that would remake their experience into a more meaningful one.

A lot of people are now creating their own video. But how do they communicate this information? The crudest method available involves the swapping of tapes. I mail you my software; you mail me yours. Effective? Yes. Satisfactory? No. Some have turned to theater events using multiple television screens and a comfortably darkened room. But this too has its limitations.

The efforts of software creators would be of minor interest were it not for the two most important developments in media: cable television and video cassettes. Here is the media revolution. A Community Antenna or Cable Television System (CATV) consists of a super antenna, a "head" which processes signals and a coaxial cable which, like the telephone cable, connects to home reception units. Subscribers pay as little as $5.00 a month for their hook-up. Present capacity is from twelve to twenty television channels through each cable, though in time, the contemplated forty-two channel hook-up projected for San Jose, California, will not be unusual. Cable now connects to 4.5 million American homes. By 1980, it is estimated that 40 percent of all American homes will be connected to cable.

Cable is radically different from broadcast TV. For one thing, the program does not travel over the airwaves, which are considered public space. Though the program is televised, the process is most analogous to telephone conversation, which suggests that an enormous variety of contents is possible within the system. The private cable owner, like Bell Tell, is in the position of renting a service for the transmission of messages without control over their content.

The possibility exists for what Paul Ryan has called "cybernetic guerila warfare." Every receiver of cable becomes a potential program originator. The implication is, and the reality may soon become, that every community will control its information. It means that the cable subscriber will have available to him a wide variety of alternatives to the one-dimensional broadcast television. It means potentially that the entire information envelope surrounding the earth will be accessible to every single human being. It means the optimum communication system: high variety of programming, low cost, built-in feedback. Finally, the introduction of video cassettes will do much to insure that not even cable regulation and government restriction will stifle the communications explosion.

Obviously, the effect of video on the arts will be dramatic. Throughout the process of technocratization, artists have chosen between two options: the first offered artists the possibility of paralleling or complementing science and the seemingly bold forces of technology, thereby playing a supportive role to the historical pattern and affirming the commitments of society. We have called this option modernism. It is a form of technological portraiture. The second option is the human resistance to the blind technocratization of the natural and human environments. This option has been characterized by Marcuse as the "Great Refusal."

Modernism anticipates an avant-garde defined by its ability to innovate, discover and change at a rate comparable with technological development; the second option pictures an avant-garde based on the artist's ability to provide a counter-cultural force—an opposition to the acculturating forces that are part of the technocratization movement. The new media will be embraced by artists of both persuasions. The media will be used to further incorporate the arts into the frozen structures of American life, as demonstrations of a modernist aesthetic, *and* the media will promote very effective counter-cultural creations. . . .

How will the new media affect art? The modernist will take to video. In fact, many of the important video developments in the past few years have been due to the discoveries of artists working with the media. The video synthesizer, Eric Siegal's colorizer, and many sophisticated techniques for use and production of ½″ videotape are attributable to the contribution of the artist. Since video is audio and visual, comprised of light and sound, artists will explore its compositional potential. To use what may prove to be a poor analogy, many artists are now painting with energy.

Video is not film. Still, used as film, it makes possible major cinematic productions because of its greater editing flexibility and erasable tape. The ability to see what you have shot without waiting three weeks for film development, and the ability to make changes, edit and mix seconds after the initial impressions are made, makes possible greater flexibility in the filmmaker's craft. But, in the end, video is electric, not chemical. It introduces feedback as an artistic variable. Feedback not only makes it possible for a viewer to experience an event or interaction, but also makes it possible for the viewer to experience his reaction to the event or interaction. And then to experience his reaction to his reaction to the event. Built into this system is the idea that the artistic event is a process, not a product. The artist's involvement with his audience is multi-dimensional. Because video greatly accelerates human time, the intensity of the experience is very great.

Video will further encourage the present shift in the arts generally to dynamic events. The new media, particularly video, use a dynamic reference. If you give a porta-pak (portable video set-up) to a novice, encourage him to shoot some tape, and then sit down and look at it, you will soon be able to demonstrate one of the most important aspects of video use. As the tape is playing back, you arbitrarily select a frame and hold it on "still." In any tape, there are dozens of still shots that are masterpieces of still-frame photography. The camera man did not try for them; it was just that by shooting reality itself within a dynamic frame, a number of excellent still-frames are recorded on the tape. If the novice using video for the first time can achieve photographic excellence, then the criteria for excellence in video must be based on a dynamic and not a still-frame aesthetic.

The neophyte video user often thinks that making video is merely a matter of acquiring a portable television unit, and entering into a world of potential software. In one sense this is correct: it is that spontaneity, that feeling of "just go and shoot it," that sense of freedom to travel, move and shoot that makes the creation of software the easeful, playful excitement that video is. Unfortunately, the neophyte *is* a neophyte because he regards his equipment as only tools and his software as finished product.

As the neophyte begins to use his camera, he may soon discover that it has many of the same properties as an eyeball. It is more than a mechanical way of recording what the eye sees; instead, it *is* an electronic eye. Not only is it capable of selecting information from the environment, but it is able to change what it sees by virtue of the electric life within it. Thus, when the camera is aimed at the monitor that shows what the camera is shooting, the video user discovers either a demonstration of infinity (the monitor showing the monitor showing the monitor . . . to infinity) or a dance of electricity seen as a wave, seen as mandala patterns, seen as electronic feedback.

The regular video camera has its limitations, generally those associated with lighting. Some video users use quartz lamps to light their subjects. Unfortunately, by adjusting to the needs of their camera, they create a studio situation which allows little interaction and spontaneity; instead it intensifies self-consciousness by requiring *people* to be *subjects*. A tivicon tube modification on the camera is one way around this. This tube intensifies light—it turns lit matches into fireballs and dark rooms into comfortable shooting situations. It is handy, visually very exciting and necessary.

The novice will also tend to regard his software as final product. Actually, any software shot becomes material for a much smaller, edited version. The edit not only records the desirable sequences of the original, but can also be used to change order, create unlikely juxtapositions, altogether refashion the original material and compress real time (the time of the interaction short) into video time (the edited tape which is shorter), which makes for much better video viewing. It is part of the video aesthetic that tape *moves,* that it has a dynamic changing quality. Unlike film, where sequences that are too long may be too long by minutes, with video, seconds count. Thirty seconds in video is a long time.

The novice may also require a structure to his work before he even begins. Rigid concepts, plot lines, shooting scripts are anathema to the experienced video user. With a general idea and the elimination of unwanted variables, the video user is apt to "let it happen," to allow spontaneity of events, assuming that if he shoots it all, he will be able to edit out those parts that he thinks unnecessary or unworthy of his final tape.

Obviously editing video is as important as shooting it. Further, with several cameras and decks on hand, one can get into a more sophisticated editing. Each time a new piece of equipment is introduced (and this must be thought of as the artist's tools) the video user finds his range of possibilities extended. With the introduction of specialized equipment like a special effects generator, which can be rented or purchased, two tapes can be overlapped or juxtaposed or used on a split screen. And here we have a new area of creative contribution—mixing. Obviously two tapes can be mixed in almost infinite ways, and the person mixing decidedly influences the nature of the final product. If the video user wishes to become still more sophisticated in his technique, he can modify the S.E.G. and make it possible to bring still more inputs into the mixing board. And if he wants to throw all caution to the winds, he can even separate and mix sound tracks.

Though a very talented video user can shoot, edit and mix his own tapes, it should be obvious by now that video does not lend itself to solos. I believe that the video media is inherently a group process. Still more fundamental is that video is inherently a process-oriented media. Though the video user creates products when it is desired to do so, or required of him, the real experience of video is in the making, the learning, the doing. It is in this sense one speaks of the media as an art form.

Group processes, as you may already know, are only as successful as the group members' ability to achieve harmony. Much of the initial work of a video team is spent learning how to learn from each other; this often occurs long before they have begun to learn what the media has to teach them. Such group efforts are fraught with numerous tensions and frustrations, but the achievement of a video team that works well together is consistently joyful. Under such circumstances, the shooting of tape, the editing, the fancy work of image juxtaposing, mixing, deciding what to include and what to reject and the realization of all of this in a final tape a number of people have made and take pride in, are the pleasures that make video a rewarding experience.

A group process, an understanding of the many parts that go

into the video process, individual excellence and group synchronism are important points to consider. A group effort in video will appeal to those who are aware that equipment is costly but vital to the extension of the powers of the video user. A group will tend to have more equipment than an individual. But it should also appeal to those who are aware that video is the communication of information—on all levels—and that how well one communicates to a large audience in part results from how well one learns to communicate to a smaller one—those you work with.

Video teams are forming all over the place. In trips to Minneapolis, Los Angeles and San Francisco, I found one or more video groups shooting tape, relating to the experiences of their community, particularly involved in dissemination of information on cable and loving every minute of it. In some cases, I saw a few portable units, lighting and the use of tape recorders for doubling on audio tracks; in other places I saw sophisticated equipment and a major emphasis on editing. But however it was done, there was the spark of enthusiasm and energy of the video user.

My remarks should not be taken to be critical of the single individual who buys a portable unit and begins shooting those tapes that seem important enough to be shot. I am only suggesting what those who have lived with video a while know—that with video it is hard to shoot the world outside without involving it and yourself in it. Fortunately, with group video processes there is almost no loss of autonomy, and there is a great gain in community.

Culturally, video completes the transition from painting to conceptual art; theater to participatory theater events; sculpture to earth works. Art and life are increasingly inseparable, and video is the most appropriate media for their joining. Under the influence of video, the arts will be encouraged to give up their elitism and learn a vocabulary that speaks to an ever-widening audience. The artist will be required to learn how to participate in dialogue. Since the gap between life experience and artistic experience is closing, the artist has both the potential for influencing mass perception and a greater danger of becoming a commodity in the entertainment business.

As a counter-cultural force, the artist can choose to fill the media with social change software, or can choose to dismantle or render ineffective (symbolically or otherwise) the existing media structures. The artist can upset structures by a political documentary (a small taste of this can be gleaned from the developments that followed Geraldo Rivera's recent exposé of Willowbrook) to the creation of experiences that provide the electronic turn-on for new life styles and life-affirming activities. Further, the artist can join with the community in the creation of an information system designed to assist self-expression, identity, control of resources and new mechanisms for democracy at the community level. The implications for educational reform as a result of artistic input with new media are enormous.

The artist can choose to become more sophisticated in the role Herbert Read assigns to him: *ein Ruttler,* an upsetter of the established order.[1] These kinds of artists will short-circuit establishment electronics. The technodadaists will be twenty-first century Robin Hoods, taking from the communications systems rich and distributing to the information poor. Right now, for example, there is a new breed of technodadaists, generally known as phone phreaks, who engage in the process of phone tripping. With "blue box" in hand, they instantaneously take control of the entire telephone system. For no other purpose than to demonstrate the single man's mastery of the electronic maze, the phone phreaks seize control of cable, satellite, and millions of telephone lines to set up their mobile underground communications network. For the Telephone Company to weed them out, they would have to spend one billion over the next twenty years in the development of a "fool" proof system. Some phone phreaks are now getting into computer raiding; they are tapping into computers with their own programs, using them for purposes other than those for which they were intended. There are even rumors that if enough phone phreaks worked together, they could bring Ma Bell to a standstill. . . .[2]

Any discussion of the new communications technology and its impact on the arts must take into account the equally probable use of the media to extend the present consolidation and control of the arts. Across the country we see the continuing institutionalization of the arts and the centralization of patronage. With the integration of the arts into the mainstream of American life, with the

[1] Herbert Read, *Art and Alienation.* Horizon Press, 1967, p. 24.
[2] Ron Rosenblum, "Secrets of the Little Blue Box," in *Esquire Magazine,* October 1971, pp. 117–25, 222–26.

"professionalizing" of the artist, the soft underbelly of culture has been exposed. The artist is made respectable, and in the process the arts are fully devitalized. The new media will have two dramatic impacts on arts management. They will enable management to be more efficient. They will bring thousands of diverse creative activities under an electronic umbrella and further serve to castrate artistic activity. Finally, Prufrock will be able to be a highly regarded painter. And the arts will be brought closer to the popular arts by a form of techno-translation, which will cause original art activity and creation to be translated through media into devitalized carcasses for a mass audience that will eventually come to believe that the arts are no more important than the rest of the meaningless fare.

Many who bask in the cybernetic sunshine believe that the new communications technology will heal us. They are convinced that the new technology of communications is larger and more influential than those who control it; that the integrative, synergetic powers of the new media will survive the attempts of corporation heads and politicians to keep information access from the people. It is a widely held belief among techno-freaks and media heads that the electric environment is inherently positive. The individual who sees the communications technology as a tool available for use but not, assuredly, a panacea or the demonstration of fascism is considered unhip to both the techno-freaks and the Luddites.

In an age of disbelief, when nothing is to be trusted, and all enthusiasms are cons, it takes a lot to get people excited. At a time when everything is revolutionary; when World War II films of Japanese-American conflicts are played on Sony televisions in Denver, Colorado, sponsored by Datsun Cars; and when twenty years of negative China images can be reversed in one week, people no longer believe. But the young and the youthful want to believe. They want to find a way out of this madness. They want to have a vision of social change, a better world, humanity, sanity and justice. Unfortunately partial victories, tentative optimism, self-motivated enthusiasms are insufficient to break the despair that comes with impotency. They need a hype, and they, in turn, feel compelled to hype the good.

A hype is when something of substantial value is fantasized to many times its actual worth. Perhaps good ideas must be presented as the greatest ones so that they can be heard over the clamor of commercial noises. Unfortunately, those who hype are only creating situations where, in the end, the thing hyped will disappoint them, be less than a miracle, become subject to corruption, and they will then become dejected, more depressed, less able to believe in the powers of any new vision to remain free of contamination by the world they wish would die.

The flower children generation was hyped. An important youth development became "The Greening of America." The psychedelic experience was hyped; important and satisfying experiences with a few specific drugs became a vision of God, the way to the truth, the death of the ego. The Eastern religion trip is hyped; the significant and enduring wisdom of the East is turned into service to Krishna, urban yogas, and the achievement of nirvanas. We are always hyping ourselves. Each new hype comes on like it is the transforming force of the world, the dramatic departure from the past, the healing mechanism for the whole society. We become enamored, then true believers and then, with our disillusionment comes the resentment at having been betrayed. We even hype people. Marshall McLuhan is ex-hype; Buckminster Fuller is present hype; John Lilly is future hype.

While our less sophisticated fellow creatures consume new products, our intelligentsia consumes new fascinations, new ideas, new heroes, like they were so much hair dressing. The intellectual's goldmine serves as a contemporary symbol of insincerity. Believing ourselves unable to make anything happen, we sit around fantasizing the importance of what is happening without us.

My purpose in elaborating on the hype is that this article on the communications revolution must conclude by extracting the substance of communications theory from its hype. If we are to profit at all from the new communications, we must—absolutely must—reject the hype so that we can fully utilize the substance. If we continue to hype ourselves, we will toss the potential benefit of these media back to the institutions. For the hype discounts the political nature of the environment and the problematic outcome of any new tool which can be used for better control or liberation. If we discount the dirty little secret of politics, we will wind up not with Childhood's End but with Hogan's Heroes.

Unfortunately many are turning the media into a cultism.

Unable to say that here is something that is really important, something that counts, they require it to be salvation, a new vision, a panacea for a new age and a new man. Unfortunately the religious trip confuses more than it clarifies; the new media are already becoming surrounded by a vocabulary and a linguistic DMZ created by communications "experts" though incomprehensible to others. As well as jargon and evangelistic rhetoric, the new media people can be characterized by a form of intolerance called the "more electric than thou" syndrome. The vision of young men and women armed with porta-paks, standing up to America with their software, their blue boxes, or their spacy games may be exciting to some; but if we are to believe that the new media will make a difference, it will only be because the kind of long-term strategy, careful planning and post-crunch survival tactics are now being worked out.

Chapter 7

the anatomy
of cable television

Barry Schwartz and Jay-Garfield Watkins

Throughout its twenty-four-year history, cable television has developed and prospered on a grass-roots level. The use of this technology which began not as a product, but as a service, has partly been determined by the needs of the people the owners of the system wish to serve. Therefore, any discussion of cable television must take into consideration not only its technological potential, but also the unprecedented alignment of citizen groups who serve the cable as an instrument for social change, and as a means of revitalizing communication among human beings.

As well as citizen groups, product-oriented industries such as the telephone utilities, television broadcasters, and manufacturers of electronic technology see the cable as an extension of themselves. The financial and scientific interests of these industries dictate a system which supports more advanced products and therefore more commercially desirable versions of their existing technology.

These two disparate interest groups direct our attention to both man's new awareness of the importance of communication tools and the incorporation of old values in the use of new media. The past, present, and future of the development of cable television then is a paradgim of man evolving while under the influence of his existing environment.

Cable television began as a device to carry program reception to rural and isolated areas that lay outside the reception range of television stations. At a certain point within the signal range of these stations, system builders erected tall antennas that caught and amplified over-the-air signals and transported them by coaxial cable to individual homes in communities with little or no reception. Each home which received community antenna television (CATV) was connected by a feeder line to the cable for a small installation charge and thereafter paid a small monthly service rate. In many cases, homes in isolated areas that were connected to the cable got clearer reception than homes in the vicinity of the station, and they were often able to get a wider selection of channels. The next development was a logical one—to install the cables in metropolitan areas. Clearer color pictures was the advantage here, as well as the reception of additional channels.

But the possibilities of the cable were not limited to transporting broadcast signals. Inherent in the construction of the coaxial cable itself is its ability to carry many channels, far more than there are over-the-air stations to fill them. To attract more customers, the cable companies first began utilizing these additional channels for weather reports, stock market quotations, and shots of AP and UPI tickertapes. Later, when owners began to originate live local programs, again to attract subscribers, socially concerned organizations, as well as the communications industries, saw the implications of the device. An all-inclusive system, cable could not only carry network programming, but produce and transmit more diverse software of its own at very little expense. Assured of monthly subscription fees from customers, cable companies, unlike over-the-air stations, did not have to depend upon advertisers who require large audiences to sell products. The flexibility of the cable allows it to tap the content of one system and then compete with it. Obviously, this duality of service raises legal questions. Broadcasters insist CATV companies should pay copyright fees for transmitting their programs as compensation for the loss of over-the-air audiences.

At the same time that they have struggled against cable television, broadcasters, telephone companies, and other media industries have been quickly buying up old cable systems and installing new ones. The threat of competition and the large profits of even the smallest cable companies are not the sole reasons for their interest. Broadcast television transmits over-the-air in what is called the electromagnetic spectrum. This spectrum, of which television uses nearly 60 percent, has become increasingly crowded with signals of the same frequency range from other media. These frequencies are known commonly as VHF or the very high frequency waves. Two-way radio systems for taxis and delivery trucks, AM and FM radio stations, walkie-talkies, air lines, and police departments use VHF. Land vehicles are and will be demanding more space in this spectrum for their radio units. The communication satellites are expected to take an even greater share of the range in the future. For the four major television networks and their outlets to claim so much of this valuable territory has become a major issue and has created yet another problem that lies within a complicated political framework.

The Federal Communications Commission is the agency that oversees the rights to ownership of the vast communication networks in the United States. The FCC, a small governmental agency whose tasks have outgrown its resources in staff, financing, and policy, lacks an overall plan for the coordination of old and new technologies, and often is the target of attack. Headed by a small group of commissioners, it bends in contradictory directions to pressures from social organizations and interested parties in each of the competing communications industries. For example, the commission may be quite lenient with a cable television company owned by an electronic corporation that is part of the telephone complex and unyielding with a small, independently owned system.

Many communication experts see the inevitability of an entire nation being wired and the eventual conversion of all television systems from over-the-air to over-the-cable transmission. They envision an interconnecting system in which the cables would have common carrier status, as the nation's telephone lines now have. Cables would be treated as public utilities, and their owners would have no control over the content of channels. Any organization, commercial or otherwise, at standard rates, would have access to the service. However, competition among the different factions, enormous investments in older technologies, and conflicts of interest among policy-makers will no doubt long delay, and may abort, the introduction of a uniform cable system.

Already in the major metropolitan areas, CATV has run up against powerful obstacles adeptly erected by established television stations. Cable companies are even having difficulties obtaining permission from telephone authorities to string their cables on existing telephone poles.

If the potential of CATV was limited to clearer images of the same television fare we have received for the past twenty-five years, we might well leave the cable controversy to the engineers and politicians. However, more and more people are becoming aware that they have an intrinsic right to determine with whom and what they will communicate. When Alexander Graham Bell demonstrated the telephone at the Philadelphia Centennial Exposition in 1876, no one saw any need for it. At first a novelty, the telephone quickly became a necessary instrument by which man gained access to man on a *common* basis. With the introduction of radio, film, and television, communication became the interaction between the active communicators (broadcasters) who *imparted* information and entertainment to a passive mass of listener-viewers. These media, "luxuries" at their inception, created the "public" and focused attention on the public's unmanageable shadow, the society.

For two decades, commercial broadcast television has educated the nation to many of its problems and created many more. By abstracting from social situations, "managing" injustices and popularizing bad taste, it has caused the nation to suffer from a collective impotency. Until recently there has been little opportunity for the American public as groups or individuals to alter this image of themselves, except via more delayed methods such as print, mass demonstrations, and face-to-face or voice-to-voice confrontation. Community antenna television, however, offers an opportunity for the people to create their own images.

The key issue at stake for those who wish to see at least a part of the CATV system used for community purposes is public access. Three years ago, civil liberty groups formed a lobby and petitioned the FCC to open up a portion of the cable channels for public use. As a result of their efforts, the FCC recently ruled that all cable television companies in the top 100 markets had to free at least one channel for community use on a nondiscriminatory basis. In several cities such as New York, Minneapolis, and Los

Angeles, two or more channels are now open to the public. The civil liberties organizations won a decisive victory for the communities. Although at present twenty percent of American homes are hooked up to cable systems, there is every indication that by 1980 at least one-half the nation will be wired.

In an excerpt from an unpublished novel, *The Biggest, Freest TV in Town* by Pete Seeger, a character states, "The purpose of life is to live, not watch others live." America has spent twenty-five years of passive nation-watching, so much so that the communities and even the cities have become invisible to the people who reside in them. Many of these communities are not even aware of the problems that afflict them until they face a major crisis. Societal wrongs are considered national rather than community questions.

Public access groups, who see CATV as a means of local expression, organization, and communication, are springing up throughout the country. These nonprofit organizations are forming for two reasons: They protect the citizen's rights in CATV, and now they are beginning to work as facilitators and catalysts, encouraging every segment of the community to participate in confronting its problems. They are offering brief training workshops in video tape equipment and program production to groups and individuals who request it and educating minorities and the poor generally to the value of the video tape process. They believe that once the members of a community learn to participate with the medium, they will no longer be able to think of themselves as static and incapable of action. When a community or group gets feedback on itself, it changes. "Nothing ever happens in my town," is a lament that will be muffled out in dialogues between groups previously unaware of each other's existence.

Thus far, there has been no discrimination in the public's access to CATV. Observing a few regulations, such as those against the use of profanity, incitements to violence, and libelous statements on private persons, any private group or citizen may request and receive free channel time on a first-come, first-served basis. The group pays only for the tape and production costs involved in the making of their software. As this process continues and communities push for more free channels, the awe with which the individual usually confronts his communication tools—and technology in general—may give way to respect for his *own* ability to communicate with greater force.

The one drawback to present and future CATV systems for community use goes back to its noncommon carrier status. Installation charges and monthly service rates will make the poorer communities the last to receive cable television. Neighborhood outlets are the solution here, where people may gather in storefronts and meeting halls not only to watch themselves, but to use the media experience as a start to organizing positive problem-solving.

There is also much discussion of the potential of CATV to serve a specialized audience. Broadcast television programs the common denominator for a mass audience. People located outside metropolitan areas who are interested in viewing concerts, dance, serious drama, and poetry readings could now have this kind of programming on local channels set aside for the purpose. Through a combination of over-the-air signals and interconnecting cables, it will be entirely possible for someone on a farm outside Topeka, Kansas, to experience live an opening night performance of an off-Broadway play in New York City.

Entire channels devoted to instruction are now a reality in some cable areas, and there is talk of extending the service to specialized professional education. Physicians may be able to receive the latest medical developments, chemists can watch new experiments being performed, and the scholar will have first-hand exposure to lectures, discussions, and demonstrations on a variety of disciplines from experts he would never be able to encounter in person.

The survival of cable television as a medium for social change in the community is dependent upon the organization of concerned citizens to counter the private interest pressures of the various communication industries. When the average citizen has the opportunity to communicate via a medium that previously excluded him and focus attention on the problems of *human* communication, he will also be able to shake the valueless foundations on which much of the present-day technological systems sit.

CATV is certainly not the answer to all of man's problems. It does not even answer the question: What will be our prime technology of communication in the future? Scientists are suggesting that direct satellite-to-home telecasting will make CATV obsolete even before the nation is completely wired. But those who recognize the potential of two-way cable systems, which enable the subscriber to be a program originator, argue that no other medium offers such dramatic feedback properties. Futurists are predicting that the unexplored laser beam is the secret to inexpensive and abundant communication technology. It is very likely, however, that satellites will be used mostly for national distribution of programs, and that a "wired nation" is not only feasible, but essential for the immediate future. What is important here is that all interests are taken into account and that a national policy is established with regard to CATV and other systems.

With better cables, in which a hundred or more channels can be compressed, the future of communications in the United States sounds like a technocrat's dream. The home, we are told, will contain a complete communications center. Return bands on the cable will supplement the present one-way system so that an individual may impart information in a variety of forms as well as receive it. Already the Bell Telephone Company has developed the videophone, which allows callers to see as well as hear each other.

Some people feel the consequences of an extensive communications system are dangerous. Having the "world" at his fingertips could eventually cut the individual off from direct personal contact with others. They see man becoming connected to a system that requires constant response to machines. Another widespread concern is the invasion of privacy. Two-way communication systems could become an effective method of police surveillance in the home and therefore destroy individual freedom. In the wrong hands, personal data collected by computer banks could very well make privacy impossible.

Yet, those who are now organizing on the grass-roots level to promote individual and group use of TV technology see cable television as the beginning of a new human communication and of greater human involvement. Taking advantage of the simplified technology he now has, the individual may begin learning not only his responsibility to society, but gain awareness of the significance of his existence. Statements such as "Who am I to say," "What does it matter," and "Who cares what I do" will diminish in frequency as he begins to see and hear the results of his own inputs and feedback to social problems. If he starts now, the individual can be on his way to self-identity within the community.

Chapter 8

subjective
realities

Robert E. L. Masters and Jean Houston

In altered states of consciousness such as dreaming sleep, trance, or psychedelic drug states, persons may experience subjective realities much as, ordinarily, they experience their existence in the external world. Even though there may be a recognition that the reality experienced is internal, still the person may feel himself to participate with some or all of his senses in the subjective reality that dominates awareness.

Although the term is inexact, most persons may best understand the experiencing of a subjective reality as a waking dream. In the altered state, however brought about, imagination is vivified to the extent that the person, usually with eyes closed, sees clearly the subjective reality, hears, touches, and is touched, is aware of moving about, and otherwise functions as persons sometimes do in dreams. Also, as in some other kinds of dreams, the person may be a spectator only, observing the subjective reality somewhat as a film is experienced in a theater.

The possibility of experimentally giving persons access to subjective realities opens up many other possibilities for the enhancement of creativity, learning, and types of self-expression conducive

"Subjective Realities," by Robert E. L. Masters and Jean Houston. Copyright © 1973 by Robert E. L. Masters and Jean Houston. This article appears for the first time in this volume. Used by permission of authors.

The work described in this paper was carried out at The Foundation for Mind Research with the aid of funds provided by the Erickson Educational Foundation of Baton Rouge, Louisiana, and the Kleiner Foundation of Beverly Hills, California.

to healing and personality development and integration. In the following pages we will describe experiments aimed at realizing these possibilities, utilizing novel instruments to alter consciousness, and in some instances greatly accelerating mental processes as becomes possible when, in altered states, we break out of the learned tyranny of time.

Throughout history people have used altered consciousness as a gateway to subjective realities, and of course to realize other goals. Rituals, drumming, dancing, chanting, fasting, ingestion of mind-altering plant substances, these and many other means have been used to the end that visions might be obtained, or glimpses of the future, and to accomplish healings and give experiences of transcendence and ecstasy.

In our own laboratory we have worked with many of these ancient and primitive enabling procedures, and also with some other instruments and methods: "sensory deprivation" or reduction of sensory inputs; varieties of audio-visual environments; stroboscopic lights; various psychedelic drugs;[1] meditation; brain wave and muscular relaxation self-regulated by means of biofeedback training; trance states self-induced and induced by the Altered States of Consciousness Induction Device, which will be described; electrical stimulation of the brain (by attached, not implanted, electrodes); and still other means.

"CRADLE OF CREATIVITY"

The Altered States of Consciousness Induction Device (ASCID) is a tool devised and used by us to alter consciousness and so gain access to subjective realities. ASCID is essentially a metal swing or pendulum in which the research subject stands upright, supported by broad bands of canvas and wearing blindfold goggles. This pendu-

---

[1] R. Masters and J. Houston: *The Varieties of Psychedelic Experience* (New York: Holt, Rinehart and Winston, 1966; paperback: Delta, 1967). *Psychedelic Art* New York: Grove Press–Balance House, 1968. "Toward an Individual Psychedelic Psychotherapy," in B. Aaronson and H. Osmond, eds., *Psychedelics: Their Uses and Implications* (New York: Doubleday Anchor Books, 1970). These and other writings describe in detail the authors' work with mind-altering chemicals. That work was concluded more than five years ago, but it is directly relevant to the research described in this paper.

lum, hanging from a metallic frame, carries the subject and moves in forward and backward, side to side, and rotating motions generated by involuntary movements of the body of the subject. Frequently, then, a trance state ensues within two to twenty minutes, and may deepen as the spontaneous or directed experiencing of a subjective reality continues to unfold.

Our own work with ASCID over several years suggests that the main tendency of the largely *undirected* research subject is to experience "worlds" or subjective realities which are fantastic and reminiscent of fairy tales, myths, and science fiction. Sometimes religious- and mystical-type experiences have occurred. The subject's experience also may be guided, and demonstrated possibilities of problem-solving and varieties of artistic work have led us to sometimes refer to the device as a "cradle of creativity."

As an example of the very largely undirected and mythic-religious-type experience, a young college graduate in the ASCID experienced herself as dying and then as being reborn as the mythic Prometheus. After "an eternity of death" she experienced "a tremendous cosmic life force entering my body through my feet. . . . This force then traveled up my body. I had superhuman strength and powers and experienced myself to be Prometheus. I was chained to the side of a rock on a mountain. The chains did not bother me because I knew I had the strength to free myself at will." She then had a powerful emotional experience of bringing fire to mankind and to various individuals, the fire being in each case symbolic of a gift of great importance to the respective persons. With each gift, she felt a more and more intense personal fulfillment.

> "The whole experience," she wrote later, "was so positive and profound that I was in a state of total awe and wonder. . . . The effects have really been far reaching. I feel myself to be boundlessly happy and at complete acceptance and peace with myself. I see life much more clearly and on many different levels. I feel myself to be in an active connection with the harmony and unity of nature and the cosmos through a force I guess you'd call love. I think this whole new way of being comes from the realization and experience of the goodness and strength of my unconscious. . . . I think the whole experience takes on even more meaning when it is known that I knew very little about the unconscious or any experience with it, and that I knew nothing about religious experiences. Since I re-

turned home I have been doing as much reading as possible on these subjects. My reading points out even more clearly the awesome profundity of what I experienced. . . ."

Similar experiences have been observed, some more typical of classical religious experiences and appearing to meet the criteria for "authenticity" set forth by scholars of religion and mysticism. For our part, as phenomenologists, we do not evaluate but only describe, leaving others to debate ontological and metaphysical questions set aside by us as unanswerable by any known means. We do feel, however, that some of the experiences we will describe should not be dismissed as just artistic or religious fantasies. Their significance undoubtedly is greater than such a dismissal would suggest. And in some of these cases we surely are looking at processes that have been basic to art and to religion.

"SELF-CREATING" WORKS OF ART

Research subjects with whom we intend to work repeatedly are trained so that they will become familiar with various aspects of the subjective realities. For example, they are trained in *Visionary Anthropology,* a mind game we have devised that requires the subject to visit a "world" and describe for us its customs, its art, and whatever else may be of interest. The subject "lives in" this subjective reality; and as he is encouraged to look at paintings and listen to music, we require of his brain-mind to produce these works of art for his enjoyment and so that he can describe them. This is an indirect exploration of the "automatisms" familiar to students of the creative process. We also work with these automatisms directly in experiments with various types of artists.

Such work explores the creative process and the psychology of imagination, but at the same time the experiment may be used to help an author overcome problems blocking the completion of a novel or some other literary work. For example, an author in his mid-30s had been unable for almost a year to complete the final chapter of his novel. Standing in the ASCID, in trance, he was told that he would be able to just watch as the chapter appeared before him as if made into a film. He would see his characters and hear them speak, but he would only observe and not consciously create. After he had experienced the chapter in this way, he was told to remember what he had seen and heard, but now to look and listen again since his unconscious was going to provide another version of the chapter that he might prefer to the first version. This was done, and in all he experienced four such performances of the chapter. After the fourth, he urgently requested that the experiment be terminated so that he could go home and write. He worked all night and most of the next day, finishing the book. The chapter was judged by him and his publisher to be equal to other chapters in the book. By tapping a subjective reality a creative block of a year's duration was broken through.

Other novelists, in the ASCID, have been enabled to "become" one or more of their own fictional characters, and as the character participate in a realistically lived through segment of the novel. In other cases, research subjects have been told just to observe while a short play or film was performed, or a picture appeared on a canvas, or a song was sung or played. These latter examples of "musical imagery" are less familiar to most people than are visual images or even visual narrative sequences having a resemblance to various types of works of art.

Many composers of music, however, have reported experiences, frequent or occasional, of auditory musical imagery, complete or fragmentary compositions, original and equal in quality to compositions created by the person by any other means. This musical imagery is of course literally heard, just as visual images are literally seen. The imagery may be of a voice or voices singing, of a single instrument, or a combination of instruments, and even of an entire orchestra playing. In vividness the imagery may range from faint and barely audible on up to a painful loudness, again comparing with visual imagery which may be barely illumined on up to a painful "blinding light." Beethoven, Berlioz, Mozart and Wagner are among the noted composers who have experienced these "automatic" and "self-creating" works of art. In a few cases the recording of such seemingly "given" imagery has been the usual method of composition. E. T. A. Hoffmann, for example, often remarked to his friends that "When I compose I sit down to the piano, shut my eyes, and play what I hear."

EXPERIMENT IN MUSICAL IMAGERY

A research subject, a young woman in her 20s, was the published writer of several popular songs. Upon her request, she was accepted as a subject for an ASCID experiment, but she was given no information that any special task would be required of her. She had stood in the device for only one minute when her head slipped involuntarily forward, the agreed-upon signal that she was in trance and as deeply in trance as she felt she would go for the present, and that she was ready to communicate. The subject then was instructed concerning a phenomenon we have called *accelerated mental process* (AMP), but which those who identified and first worked with the phenomenon termed "time distortion."

This pioneering work was accomplished by Linn Cooper and Milton Erickson and described by them in a book published in 1954.[2] The authors were hailed at the time as having opened up the way to possible major breakthroughs in creativity, psychotherapy, and possibly learning. However, research has been limited, and even this has been discouraged by the usual complaints that the phenomenon must be invalid because it fails to improve the learning of nonsense syllables.

In the case of our subject, she was now instructed that in a trance, as in dreaming sleep or drug states, it is possible to greatly increase the rate of thought or amount of subjective experience beyond what is ordinarily possible within a given unit of clock-measured time. For example, in trance, a person might experience within a few minutes as measured by the clock such a wealth of ideas or images that it will seem to him hours, or days, or even longer must have passed for so much to be experienced. But only a few minutes of objective time have elapsed; the change has been on the level of subjective, experiential time; and the explanation lies in the phenomenon of AMP.

Following this explanation, an illustration of AMP revivification of experience was provided. She was told that she would now

[2] Linn F. Cooper and Milton H. Erickson: *Time Distortion in Hypnosis* (Baltimore: Williams & Wilkins, 1954).

find herself back at a stadium where, a few days before, she had observed a football game. She would be given three minutes of clock time, and this would be quite sufficient, with AMP, for her to subjectively see the game through from beginning to end. Nothing would seem hurried, all would be as before, but the several hours of subjective experience would occur within the amount of clock time given. When, at the end of three minutes, the subject was asked to report, she said that she had seen the game in its entirety and had been waiting for a while alone in the stadium, everyone else having left.

The subject then was told: "Now you are going to find yourself walking down a street in a city on a misty evening, and you will feel the mist and smell the odors of the street and hear the street noises, and you will be aware of your body, a little tired, as you walk, and of wanting to have something to eat and drink. You will find yourself approaching a little cabaret, and go inside and order for yourself a sandwich and some beer, and while you are sitting there a singer will come out and perform. The songs she will sing will be ones you have never heard before, and they will be songs that you like. You will stay listening to her just as long as you want to, and you will commit these original songs to memory. You will have all the time you need to do this, staying for an hour or however long you want, and you will need only two minutes of clock time for these things to happen."

Asked if she understood, the subject smiled and said she was already enjoying the beer and sandwich and was waiting for the singer. She was told: "You have two minutes, starting *now!*" After a little less than two minutes, she asked, "Well, do you want to hear the song?"

The subject then sang for us a very pleasant song, complete with lyrics, and after that announced she had two others, which she also sang, apologizing when she felt she had forgotten some of the lines. Asked if she had ever heard or thought about any of the songs before, she said that two were definitely new to her but possibly one line of the other song was something she had thought about before. Asked her opinion of the songs, she said that one was complete but the other two might require some additional work to be ready for publication. All of the songs were of the sort she had written in the past—pleasant, sentimental tunes.

Two more similar experiments were carried out, and more songs were produced by the subject. Since all of these songs might have been already created by the subject, but preconscious, it was decided to elicit from her music quite unlike any of her usual compositions. As we were about to begin, however, she complained that she was tired of standing for so long in the ASCID. The goggles and supporting straps were removed, and the subject was told to "Bring your trance with you over to the couch." She lay down, reporting her state of consciousness to be unchanged, and experimental work was resumed.

"Now," she was instructed, "you will find yourself on a path in a jungle with huge, lush plants and trees overhead and moonlight filtering down through. Move along that path on a warm night in the jungle, not being afraid but moving as a sleepwalker, slowly being drawn towards something, you don't know what. (Here she interrupted to say that she was moving down the path.)

"Until you come to a clearing, and inside of that clearing a ritual is being performed. There are bodies glistening, a fire leaping in the center of the clearing, people dancing, drums beating, a very wild, primitive kind of scene. But it all expresses and creates a oneness . . . an extremely wild, primitive, frenetic sort of music, forging a collective consciousness among those who are participating in the ritual. Completely primitive. I want you to listen to this, to absorb it, to be able to sing it, and it will be a kind of music that can create a primitive unity of consciousness among those who hear it. Listen to them, look at them, feel what they're feeling. The message will be oneness in *their* terms. You have one minute of clock time, but that will be enough for you to stay with them for as long as you like, and that clock minute begins *now!*"

At the end of the minute the subject, reporting herself to be still quite elated, sang for us a very wild and effective chant that continued for several minutes. She then was asked to tell us about what she had experienced:

> At first I was standing off to one side, kind of watching and making mental notes about what they were doing. Then I was doing it with them because it was a sound that just went all around and in me and out of me. I was doing it with them and they were dancing. My body wasn't dancing but it was into all the rhythms that they were into. Then they were sitting. There was a silence and they all

sat, they all fell down kind of, they didn't sit slowly, but instead
they all fell down into sitting positions. They all kind of curled
themselves up into themselves and put their heads down. Everybody
had their eyes closed but it didn't matter, you didn't have to look
or touch anybody because the feeling was just all over, in the ground
and the sky and everything. This feeling, it was just part of the
ground and the sky and the people, you know, there just wasn't
any you and me and world around. I was just one with them and
they were all one voice and one breathing together. At first I was
frightened, because they already were into it when I got there, but
then pretty soon I was where they were. But not right away, because they were really, really far, far out. . . . Once before, in
group chanting, I experienced something a little like this, but then
there was a lot more mind in it. This was all body and skies and
earth, and then it wasn't really people. For a while you couldn't
experience it as a "we," because there was just a one. Then it
wasn't even human, it was just a physical being that I was part of.

At the conclusion of these experiments, the subject said that
she was fascinated and pleased, but felt a little guilty, "as if I have
just been eavesdropping on some other reality and didn't really
create anything." But, she added, "If I didn't create that music, then
who did create it?"

The question she raises is one that has interested artists and
students of genius and the creative process for centuries. Once assumed to be gifts from the gods, automatisms are now generally
attributed to a creative unconscious, whatever that might be. Those
who experience the phenomenon are often, even more than others,
impressed by the feeling that the work has been "given," not created
by them. Even so astute a psychologist of the creative process as
Nietzsche felt obliged to grapple with the question of who or what
had provided him with his *Zarathustra*.

To say the least, it must seem remarkable to encounter some
unconscious process able to create according to specifications and
providing for consciousness music to be heard as auditory images
and sung by cabaret singers, primitives, or perhaps played by an
orchestra. The same process, manifesting in a trance or psychedelic
drug state, and complying with suggested AMP, has been observed
by us to almost instantaneously provide fictional or dramatic works,
or at least fragments thereof, and images of paintings or sculptures.
It may equally well be enlisted for problem-solving or psychotherapy.

AMP AND LEARNING

With accelerated mental process (AMP), or "time distortion," it appears to be possible to very quickly and dramatically learn, or perhaps rehearse and apply learnings which were previously ineffective, and to do this within the context of a subjective reality.

For example, a Jesuit priest felt that he had been "traumatized" by his experience of a thirty-day "retreat" during which he had failed in succeeding to realize many of the tasks and objections of the Jesuit spiritual exercises. In three minutes of trance, and with AMP, he relived the entire thirty days but, this time, "paid very close attention," applied his knowledge gained from listening so closely, and completed the exercises very successfully. Afterwards, he was relieved of what he considered to be symptoms produced by the trauma, and he felt more self-assured, much more at ease with other people, and more creative. With respect to the latter, he was able to produce and have published a series of papers he had long planned but been unable to write.

In another case, a young art student worked as a research assistant for the authors, and demonstrated an ability to self-induce deep trance states. She participated in many kinds of experiments, and displayed an unusual ability to regulate her own states of consciousness and so disinhibit capacities when required for a particular task. She was not, however, improving as an artist, and she requested that an experiment be devised to enable her to better make use of the talent and skills she believed herself to have.

It was agreed that this would be attempted, and she was asked to go outside and execute a drawing. She returned with a crude sketch of some branches to which, in the upper left corner of the paper, she added a drawing of her foot. She then, upon request, went into a deep trance and was told that she would now study with a very fine art teacher, and that she would carefully learn and apply the instruction she was going to receive. On this occasion, she would receive a full day's instruction and for this only five minutes of clock time would be required. At the end of this period, she came out of the trance and expressed surprise that daylight was still coming through the window. She was sent outside to make another sketch of the same vine-covered branch she had drawn a little earlier. In about thirty minutes she returned, showing us a sketch that was clearly a considerable improvement over her first effort, and that showed a previously lacking ability to work in detail.

For the next two days, the subject was given several more five-minute intervals, each to be experienced as a full day of art instruction. At the end of each of these sessions she was given some object to draw, and a continuing, definite improvement in her work was noted.

Five days from the date of the first experiment, the subject was requested to go into a deep trance and then was told that she now would have the opportunity to study for an entire semester with her art teacher. She would study drawing, she would learn a great deal, she would work very hard, and she would be able to live through the entire semester within thirty minutes of clock time.

At the end of thirty minutes, the subject was wakened but insisted that she must go back into trance to complete a "great drawing" she was working on when interrupted. She was told, however, that it now was time for her to execute that drawing on real paper and in the waking state. She agreed, but said a large sheet of paper was required, and urgently asked that it be obtained at once. When we found drawing paper to meet her needs, she asked to return home immediately so that she could get to work. She then worked intensely for most of two days and, at the end of that time, had completed a drawing that evidenced skills well beyond any to be seen in her previous work.

In this drawing, the tree and vines that had figured in the first two drawings are retained as segments of an elaborate fantasy. The work is very crowded, as often happens when an artist executes a work conceived during AMP experiments. The work also is expressive of conflicts, and served to exorcise some of these. The drawing was experienced as a major creative breakthrough, and the subject has preserved her gains and has continued to improve during the eighteen months since the experiment was completed. Her work not only is technically much better, it is more sophisticated, original, also more simple and serene. The subject's own comments written a few months after the experiment include the following summary and evaluation of results:

> Being in a very deep trance I was told that I would experience a one-semester drawing course. During this course I would have a master teacher at my side whenever he was needed, and I would do all that was necessary to fulfill the course requirements.
>
> I have an unusually poor recollection of this session. However, I do know that I produced a very large number of drawings, some of them being done time and again until perfect. Also, that many things were happening in my head besides just drawing. I can still see myself coming and going to class, and know that at the time I must have lived life in a normal way throughout that one semester. And so, it seems that the time that passed within my mind was several months.
>
> At the end of the course I had done many drawings. It was quite evident that my skill had greatly improved because of all the practice I had had. Of these drawings I was to choose one and, while out of trance, actually reproduce it. This I did. My drawing has no name, I do not even know what it might mean. But it is a statement of what was seen and worked out during my course.
>
> . . . Directly following the last session I was physically exhausted. My head felt as if there was no way my neck could ever support it. It felt just as if it had been stretched, and when put back into shape another 50 pounds or so had been added. Also, it pounded a bit, something which must be known as a headache to others, but something I had only experienced once or twice before. These adverse effects were gone as soon as I slept.
>
> The value of the session has lived on. The drawing itself is an example. My art teacher could hardly believe that I had done the drawing, and I, too, am surprised. As far as my talent goes, I am (or, rather, was) extremely wild and undisciplined. I never finished anything. However, since that drawing I have improved almost too much to be conceivable. My work is now disciplined and carefully thought out. Shading has reached a more advanced level, and my work is so much more creative. I am now on the threshhold of another stage of development—at last I am able to draw from within me, rather than just copying the naturalistic world which can be seen all around. I feel much more contented to be drawing what cannot be seen by all.

It is very difficult to assess such experiments and hope to determine whether anything was learned and, if so, in what sense something new might have been learned. It is also difficult to say whether the improvement has resulted from the overcoming of a creative block or, if not that, what the cause of the improvement may have been. Neither can we hope to measure the amount of experience lived through by the subject. Much more research is needed, but what is clear is that mental processes may be accelerated and that this acceleration may be very great within the context of a subjective reality. Results make it undeniable that AMP within a subjective reality sometimes provides the means to approach with good likelihood of success various tasks, creative objectives, and psychotherapeutic goals.

IMAGE MEDITATION: DEATH-REBIRTH

The most effective known means for changing values and for transforming personality remains the religious or mystical experience, however induced and whatever name employed to describe it. Even approximations to the more profound experiences of these kinds may be emotionally very powerful and beautiful. Potent psychic energy sources may be tapped, and there may be an activation of healing and growth mechanisms that apparently have to be triggered or disinhibited before becoming active in behalf of the person. Here we will describe an experiment that often yields emotionally powerful approximations to the most profound experiences aimed for by the various spiritual disciplines. These experiences, also of subjective realities, may in addition bring individuals close to realities traditionally termed ultimate. In any case, they should be of considerable interest to psychotherapists and scholars of both art and religion, as well as to psychologists exploring the creative process and religious experience.

The experiment is done with both individuals and groups. Research subjects are told to close their eyes and to pay no attention to the world around them, except for the experimenter's voice. As consciousness moves deeply inward, they are told, they will see a series of images, and each of these images, successively, will be a symbol representing the person. Each successive symbol will be more profound than the last and more comprehensive. Finally, a symbol will emerge that is the most profound and comprehensive of all, and the person then should hold in mind and meditate upon that symbol.

When some time has elapsed, we next tell the subjects that they are going to experience something that can be very powerful, a symbolic death and rebirth. To achieve this, they should observe the self symbol very, very closely. As they observe it, the symbol will grow smaller, smaller and dimmer, until at last it disappears. Then the person will experience death, and, after that, when death has been known fully, there will be a rebirth. Subjects are told that they do not have to have this experience, but that it is now available to them if they do want to have it.

In one group experiment the subjects were members of a class taught by one of the authors. The course was in "Phenomenology of Religious Experience," and the experiment was conducted to enable students to better understand the experiences written about by such authors as William James and Evelyn Underhill. It was perhaps the first—but should be by no means the last—example of a course offering "field trips" in experiential and subjective realities.

Members of this college course selected to participate were eight young women, ages 21 to 25. Two of them later described the death-rebirth experience as follows:

The first subject's self-symbol emerged as "a circle which soon changed form and became a curved sea shell, the kind you can listen to. I watched it become filled with spirit which created itself anew as flesh . . . I understood the symbol immediately: the round receptivity of a shell, its emptiness to spirit. The significance of the shell's transformation into flesh—into softness and sensitivity—was obvious. As the symbol became smaller, there was a heightening of intensity and emotion. I experienced fear of the death process, which was grasped as a loss of so much of self that destruction and creation appeared terrifyingly one. . . . Everything appeared possible and impossible at once. . . . I was filled with an unquenchable desire and fear before the death-rebirth event.

"I remember being in the throes of death and not knowing what my outcome would be. This not-knowing was central to my choice to surrender to death. As I experienced myself rising from the depth of death, I knew that the gift of life was before me, and I reached out for it. I was filled with an ecstatic relief and acceptance that seemed to embrace my whole being. Then I felt as if my spirit were being quickened and reformed and was pulsing within. After that, an intense passivity and sense of being filled. I became aware of the tears on my cheek which had come during the struggle."

The second subject's symbol was a circle filled with white fire. As she observed it, "The circle became smaller and smaller, drawing my vision of it to a tiny velvet line. It finally disappeared and I felt myself go totally silent in waiting. Then there was a tremendous slow motion kind of explosion and upsurge and outgo of energy all around and from the point where the light disappeared. It was incredible. Then the circle grew and grew to infinite proportions within me, and all the sound was white. It was a silent Beethoven symphony throbbing all over the place. All the colors in the world were transformed in the whiteness and alive glow of this fire. . . . I grew huge and transparent, filled and permeated with the light and fire. And I thought: My God is a God of Love and He lives within me.

"When I opened my eyes the whole room was living brown, then as I shifted my vision from the wood to the books and the ceiling, I was part of all there was, yet wholly myself. Beautiful is all I can say."

EXTERNAL STIMULI-SUBJECTIVE REALITY

In some other experiments, an audio-visual environment is used by us to induce altered states of consciousness, and as an example of the incorporation of external stimuli into subjective realities.

The audio-visual environment used in the experiments to be described here was originally created with the invaluable assistance and guidance of Don Snyder, a leading multimedia and lumia artist. In this environment, slides are projected over the surface of an 8-by-8-foot semicircular rear projection screen behind which the subject is sitting. The subject sits up close to the curved screen, so that the images occupy his entire field of vision, and he has the feeling of almost being "in" the slide projection. Sound, most often electronic music, but also sometimes Sufi or Zen chanting, comes to the subject through headphones or from speakers situated at each side of him.

The visual program consists of dissolving 2-by-2-inch slides, projected by two projectors over the entire surface of the screen. The program is exactly repeatable since the sound tape controls at pre-programmed intervals both the changing of the slides and the flexible (1 to 20 seconds) duration of the slide dissolves. Most of the audio-visual programs consist of from 120 to 160 slides and are of from 30 to 45 minutes duration.

The slides, each one an original painting, painted with transparent colors on 2-by-2-inch squares of glass, are abstract and intended either to elicit specific emotional and projective responses or to facilitate and encourage free projection—a "seeing into" the abstraction which itself is as free of suggestive materials as possible.

As ordinarily worked with, the audio-visual environment induces a mild altered state of consciousness or trance, and in a minority of cases much more profoundly altered states, or deep trances. Characteristic responses include such phenomena as time disorientation, empathy, anxiety, euphoria, body-image changes, religious and erotic feelings, projected imagery, pronounced relaxation, feelings of mild intoxication, a strong sense of wanting to go, or being drawn into, the image. The following description by a woman in her 70s is fairly typical of what might be experienced by a responsive, but not exceptionally responsive, subject:

> As I sat behind the screen watching all those colors and abstract designs whirl and swirl and dissolve into each other continuously I had no idea what they were supposed to do to me. It was a strange, bewildering, slightly frightening experience but pleasurable, incredible, awesome, like watching the Northern Lights I saw once, or it was like being a witness at the beginning of the world. Then it felt like the chaos of the modern world and of abstract art. The sounds in the earphones on my head were mostly unpleasant, my eyes and ears were being bombarded. It was impossible to think.
>
> I began to feel uncontrollably sleepy. I wanted to succumb and go to sleep but doubted if that would be of any use to you. Therefore I forced myself to remain awake. . . . When you came for me at the end I arose, and I had no concept of how long I had been there—it seemed like a very long time and yet like a few minutes. I was amazed to discover that I could scarcely walk, my limbs were so heavy, my mind in a pleasant but disoriented state. I recall I said, "I feel as if I've had five champagne cocktails."

An exceptionally strong sensory response was made to the same program by a female subject in her early 20s, setting the stage for a subsequent and unique experiment. Her remarks are made just following the audio-visual stimulation:

Wow! I craved it, really craved it, and wanted more, especially more touch sensations. I was getting the most touch when the music was loudest, and there were sort of erotic sensations that got more intense when there were dots on the screen. . . . At first I was just looking at it, but soon I was taking part, feeling the rhythms all through my body. I put my head back to try to breathe better and began breathing through my mouth rather than through my nostrils, breathing hard, especially at a crescendo when everything was throbbing. Toward the end I didn't notice anything because I was feeling so much. . . .

I felt crucified, was thoroughly exhausted but wanted more. At one point I was extremely tense, then it got delicate again with softer colors. At another point I was seeing lots of eyes, phallic forms, wombs, circles, openings, things to be pierced. The sensations got very erotic. . . . Sometimes, I would start rocking. I often wanted to close my eyes and just fall in. . . . At some point, I stopped thinking and just *was*. . . . It was so profound, the craving for more, my whole body was just aching for it.

The subject also mentioned that her sense of time was "lost," and she repeatedly emphasized that the music was not just heard, but was experienced as tactile sensations and as "intense physical vibrations."

In the case of the subject being described, her very intense sensory-erotic response to the audio-visual program was recalled by us a year or so later when we were considering a novel experiment to demonstrate one of various means by which mystical-type experiences might be enabled to occur. The subject by this time had worked with us repeatedly and was an excellent deep trance subject, although she disliked the notion of hypnosis and usually required that trance be induced by placing her in the ASCID. If that was not feasible, she would agree to imagine herself to have been placed in the ASCID, whereupon a deep trance would immediately result.

In preparation for the planned experiment, the subject, in deep trance, was given one minute, with accelerated mental process, in which to reexperience the audio-visual environment. She reported having done this, and gave a description of her responses that was almost identical to the one recorded earlier. She then was told that at some future date she would physically go into the audio-visual environment, and she then would respond as she had done the first time, and as she had done again a moment ago, only on this future occasion all of her responses would be much more intense, and it also might be that the most pleasurable of her responses would be experienced as being of extremely long duration. She was told she would have a post-trance amnesia for these instructions, but, without remembering, would carry out the instructions on the occasion of the experiment, whenever it might take place.

Several months after this suggestion was given, the subject was placed in the audio-visual environment where she experienced a loss of ego boundaries in the perceptual sphere, although an incomplete ego dissolution with respect to awareness of self. She declared that what had happened was indescribable, but that she would tell about it as best she could. The experience had been extremely pleasurable for her, and might be called a kind of *esthetic* mystical experience. Excerpts from her verbal report follow:

> It's the images and colors that take you into it. Then, "colors" is the wrong thing to say, because you stop making identifications in the sense that you recognize "blue" as in a separate category of experience. I had the sense that there was only one color—not that I was seeing monochromatically, but the colors were all just color. . . . And it was without any sense of an environment, or it felt as though all the environment was my own body. . . . I just can't describe it, but I feel obliged to produce for you, and as soon as I say it I know that I haven't been able to produce anything that really mirrors what happened. . . . I'm also not wanting to give the impression that I picked up a drug store copy of some book on mysticism that says "all is one." See, this is not on a *theoretical* level that I am speaking, not on a level of abstraction that says we all are one. . . . What I am talking about is an actual *sensory* experience. I want to convey how it felt, and it was a total, actual experience.

Essentially, this experiment was based upon the observation that prolonged and intense sensory stimulation may result in a mystical-type experience, and that the experience will be pleasurable if the sensory stimuli are pleasurable ones. Such an approach to mystical experience might perhaps be called body-mind affirmative, as distinguished from other, more common approaches taking the *via negativa*, or ascetic path of obliteration, the traditional mystic's way.

CONCLUSION

The authors have described some experiments involving altered states of consciousness and subjective realities. Some of the experiences mentioned have obvious value and pragmatic applications, while others are explored more to obtain basic knowledge that may lead to productive applications in the future. The experiments open up areas of experience which many people have thought to be largely inaccessible, or accessible only by such means as mind-altering drugs or very lengthy and arduous dedication to spiritual disciplines.

One reason why so little has been done to realize many of the mind's potentials, is that experiences such as some of those we have been describing always tend to be either overvalued or undervalued. They tend to be regarded with superstitious awe, dismissed as "airy nothings," or they are feared because of superficial resemblance to some experiences of psychotic persons. Human potentials will begin to be more fully realized when psychologists, psychiatrists, and others have ceased to be so fearful of the mind, while retaining respect for the mind.

A truly rational approach to the nonrational is one of the most urgent needs of mankind, and a true collaboration of reason with imagination would open the way to realization of much more fully human personalities, with many personal and interpersonal conflicts resolved in a greater creativity available for the benefit of all.

Chapter 9

i can't believe
i saw
the whole thing!

Isaac Asimov

In 1971 the Nobel Prize for physics went to Dennis Gabor, a Hungarian-born British subject now working in America. He had earned the award in 1947, nearly a quarter-century before, by inventing a process of recording images in a way that reproduced far more information than could be done by any other technique known. Because it contains virtually all the information, Gabor named the process "holography," from Greek words meaning "the whole message."

For sixteen years the process and the name slumbered in technical journals. Then in 1963 two electrical engineers at the University of Michigan, Emmett N. Leith and Juris Upatnieks, carried the Gabor technique a step further and made the front pages of newspapers.

Where Gabor had worked with electron waves and had applied his technique to improving the images formed by electron microscopes, Leith and Upatnieks applied the techniques to light. Using the then newly developed laser, they produced a transparent sheet of film that was grayish in color, like an underexposed photographic film, and used it to form a three-dimensional image in remarkably fine detail, and they did it without lenses.

How was it done?

To begin with, let us consider photography, a process that is by now quite familiar to us (though when it was first developed over a century ago it seemed just as mysterious to the general public).

Photography depends on the ability of light to initiate certain chemical changes. Without going into detail, we can say that light causes a colorless solution of a certain type to precipitate tiny black granules. If the solution is mixed with gelatin, coated on a film, and allowed to dry, the entire film will turn dark if it is exposed to light briefly and then treated with appropriate chemicals.

Suppose, however, that the film is exposed to light only indirectly, that the light is allowed to shine on some object, and that only the portion of the light that is reflected off the object in the proper direction strikes the film. Some parts of the object will reflect light more efficiently than other parts will; some parts will reflect light directly toward the film, while other parts direct the light more or less away from the film; some parts will scatter the light that falls on them, sending it in many directions, while others will reflect the light without scattering.

The result of these differences in detail is this: The reflected beam of light will possess fine differences in brightness from point to point. When such a reflected beam of light enters our eyes, the pattern of varying light and dark is turned into a pattern of electrical impulses in the optic nerve. Our brain interprets the pattern in such a way as to give us an idea of the shape, the color, the texture, and so on, of the object that has reflected the light. We "see" the object.

But what if the same reflected beam of light falls on the photographic film? The pattern of varying brightness in the beam would then reproduce itself on the film. At a point on the film where there impinges a portion of the light beam that is quite bright, a considerable amount of chemical change is induced. Upon proper treatment, that point becomes dark indeed. Where there impinges a dim portion of the light beam, there is little chemical change and that part of the film remains light.

Producing a proper pattern on the film requires that the film be enclosed in a box. This prevents light from striking the film from anything other than the object we want to record. Also, from each point on the object a sheaf of reflected light fans out. If all this light entered the opening in the box, each part of the film would be subject to some light from every part of the object and the result would be a featureless blurring of the entire film. To prevent this, a lens is placed in the opening. Light passing through the lens is collected into a focus and brought to the film in an orderly fashion. (The light-recording part of the eye, the retina, is also enclosed in a "box," the eyeball; and behind the eye's opening, the pupil, there is also a lens.)

The light focused on the film by the lens in the camera produces an image of the object that reflected the light—but in reverse. The brighter portions of the beam are recorded as dark spots on the film and the dim portions as light spots. The result is a "photographic negative."

If featureless light is made to shine through a photographic negative so that the light falls on a fresh film, the process is reversed again. All the dark places on the negative produce a dim portion of the beam passing through and are recorded as light places on the new film, and vice versa. The new result is a "photographic positive" that records the light-and-dark pattern of the beam exactly as it was reflected from the object.

If certain dyes are added to the film, advantage can be taken of the fact that some objects reflect light of particular wave lengths. If three images are superimposed on the film, each involving a different wave length of light, a photographic positive is produced that shows color rather than a mere dark-and-light pattern.

Assuming that the photography has been properly conducted, that the proper amount of light has entered the camera, and that the lens has been properly focused, one "sees" the object on the film as in reality, and the image is recorded for as long as the film endures.

But is the image really *exactly* like the reality? No, not really. Actually, the aspect of reality that the photographic image produces is quite incomplete. Suppose you look at an object—say two chessmen on a chessboard—through a small rectangular picture frame so as to make the object and its surroundings appear similar to the photographed image on the rectangular film. What then are the differences between the real object and the image? (Of course, you can touch and feel the real object and not the photographic image, but let us confine ourselves to visual properties only.)

Clearly it is possible to tell image from reality by vision alone.

Suppose you shift your head slightly as you look at the real object through the frame. What you see also shifts. From one position, the nearer chessman may obscure the one behind it; but as you move your head, the farther chessman seems to move out somewhat from behind the closer one. You see the real object in three dimensions and can look around an obstacle by moving your head.

This is not possible with the film. The film may give an illusion of three dimensions; a more distant object will look smaller than a similar object that is closer; the lines of a chessboard may show perspective. Still, however clever the photographic image, the appearance of three dimensions remains an illusion and nothing more. No matter how you shift the position of your head, the image that you see never changes. You see one view and one view only.

Another difference is this. In looking at a real setting, you can focus your eyes on a nearer object, leaving a farther one out of focus, or, in reverse, you can focus on the farther at the expense of the nearer. You can move back and forth at will from one focus to the other. The image has a single focus. If the farther chessman is photographed a bit out of focus so that the nearer one is clear and sharp (or vice versa), nothing you can do with your eyes can bring the out-of-focus portion into focus.

The reason for these limitations of the ordinary photograph is that it is the recording of the intersection of the light pattern with a flat, featureless surface (the photographic film). The intersection, not surprisingly, has the properties of a flat surface, and in the process the reflected beam of light loses all its three-dimensional information. Photography ("the light message") is not holography ("the whole message").

But suppose you record the intersection of the light pattern with something more complex than a featureless, flat surface. Suppose you record the intersection of the light pattern with *another light pattern*.

A beam of light consists of very tiny waves. The pattern in a beam exists because some light waves have a greater amplitude than others do (they move farther up and down). This means the pattern is brighter in some places than it is in others. The pattern also exists because some light waves are longer than others, which means that the pattern shows different colors from place to place.

If two beams of light cross each other at an angle, particular waves in one beam may happen to match particular waves in the other. Both waves move up and down together. The result is that they reinforce each other. In combination the two move up and down farther than either would separately. The combination of waves is brighter than either alone would be.

In this way, when two patterns cross, the waves interfere with each other to form a new pattern of light and dark that wasn't present in either of the two original patterns. The new pattern is called an "interference pattern."

If you have an interference pattern, you can, in theory, work out two patterns that could, in combination, form the interference pattern. The trouble is that any of an infinite number of combinations could have formed the interference pattern and that there would be no way of deciding exactly which combinations did the job in reality.

Of course, if you knew one pattern of the two that formed the combination, you could calculate the other. To do this most easily, however, you would want the known pattern to be as uniform as possible. If one beam of light were simply uniform from one side to the other, with no variations in brightness or color, then the pattern of the other beam could be determined from the resultant interference pattern.

But how are we going to get a beam of uniform light—a "reference beam"? Ordinary sunlight won't do. Sunlight might look blank and patternless, but it consists of a mixture of many colors of light waves in a whole range of wave lengths. To work out the components of an interference pattern, where the simpler of the combining beams is as complicated as apparently featureless sunlight, is impractical.

But how about producing a single color of light by heating some chemical substance that will then emit a single wave length of light? Even that is not enough, for some of the light waves go in one direction, some in another. Even a beam of ordinary monochromatic (one-color) light is not really featureless.

In fact, when Dennis Gabor first worked out the techniques of using interference patterns, there was no conceivable way these techniques could be employed for light waves. Nowhere, either in nature or in the laboratory, did a beam of light exist in which all the waves were of exactly the same length and moving in exactly the same direction. Unless such a beam could be found or could be made, there was no reference beam blank enough to allow us to calculate the pattern of the other beam with certainty from the interference pattern of the two. Gabor used his technique for waveforms other than light waves where a calculation could be made.

But then in 1960 the American physicist Theodore Howard Maiman constructed the first laser. The laser is a device that produces a powerful beam of light in which all the waves are of exactly the same length and in which all the waves move in exactly the same direction. At last the truly blank reference beam existed. The laser beam contains no pattern, no "information." When it crosses a reflected beam, all the information in the interference pattern can be referred to the reflected beam alone.

Suppose, then, we set up a situation as follows. A laser beam is made to shine obliquely on a piece of glass that is so treated as to allow half the beam to pass through, while the other half is reflected. The half of the beam that passes through continues to travel in a straight line until it passes through a rectangular opening. The half of the beam that is reflected strikes some object, and some of it is reflected again in such a way as to pass through the same rectangular opening.

The original laser beam (without a pattern) crosses over the richly patterned reflected beam and produces an interference pattern. All the information of the interference pattern would refer to the pattern of the reflected beam. If you were to look through the opening from the other side, you would see the object clearly despite the interference pattern formed with the laser beam.

However, instead of allowing the eye to look through the opening, suppose we put a photographic film in the opening. In that case a photograph will be taken of the interference pattern. All the light and dark areas will be recorded. The pattern would be so fine, however—the alternate patches of light and dark so tiny—that nothing would be visible to the eye. The film would merely take on a slight grayness.

The successfully exposed and fixed film, carrying the interference pattern, is a "hologram."

Now suppose that a laser beam is made to shine on the hologram at the same angle as the original laser beam when the hologram was formed. The laser beam illuminates the same interference pattern that had been set up when, originally, it had crossed the reflected beam. (Techniques had been developed whereby ordinary white light can be substituted for laser light at *this* stage.)

If you look through the hologram illuminated by the laser beam, matters will be exactly the same (from the visual angle) as when you looked through the opening previously. You will see the object as if it were actually there. You will see it in its actual size, its actual appearance, and even its actual three-dimensional characteristics. The hologram is the whole message.

If, through the hologram, you are looking at the image of the two chessmen, one partly behind the other, and you move your head in one direction, you will see less of it. Furthermore, you can focus on the nearer chessman, allowing the rear one to go somewhat out of focus.

Of course, you can't do more to the image than you could do to the real object; it would be unreasonable to expect to do so. When you look at the real object through a rectangular opening, there is a limit to how far you can see around an obstacle. If you move your head too far in one direction or another, you can move yourself out of the range of vision through the opening. The hologram fixes the opening, and you can't move beyond it. In the case of the real image, you can move around and behind it to look at its rear but only at the expense of getting entirely away from the opening. Therefore, you can't do that in the case of the holographic image.

Then, too, you can expect no surprises in a single *photograph* of a holographic image. A photograph taken of such an image is only a photograph, quite two-dimensional, and in itself has no holographic properties. However, you can take different photographs of the same holographic image; you can take photographs at different focuses and from different angles. The individual photographs may be ordinary, but a number of them taken together will give you a hint of the versatility of the holographic image.

There are some important ways in which a hologram, which has recorded an interference pattern, differs from an ordinary photograph that has recorded a flat intersection of a reflection pattern. For one thing, there is no such thing as a hologram negative or a hologram positive. If all the white-and-dark areas of an interference pattern were reversed, it would still be the same interference pattern carrying the same information.

Then, too, a hologram is recorded without a lens. Different parts of the interference pattern are not focused on different parts of the hologram. Instead, every portion of the hologram is bathed in the crossing over of the two beams of light so that the interference pattern is recorded again and again on every part of the hologram.

If you cut a hologram in half, you are *not* left with two halves of a complete picture. Each half of the hologram can be used to produce the complete holographic image. If you tore the hologram into ten ragged pieces, each piece could be used to produce the complete holographic image. If you scratched the hologram, the part actually scratched would be spoiled, but all the rest would still produce the complete holographic image with no signs of a scratch upon it. If you punched a hole in the hologram, you would still get an image with no sign of a hole. Dust upon the hologram would not interefere either, because the portions not covered by dust particles would still do the work.

There is, however, a limitation.

The interference patterns on the different parts of the hologram—actually repetitions of the same pattern—reinforce one another. The more repetitions there are of the pattern, the sharper and clearer the image is. As the hologram is torn into smaller and smaller pieces, or as it is subjected to more and more holes and scratches or to a thicker and thicker dust cover, the dimmer and fuzzier the image becomes.

You can see this if you imagine someone writing his name with a very light pressure on a hard pencil and with a very shaky stroke. The name may be too dim and shaky to make out. If he repeats the process, though, writing his name over and over again in the same place, there will be repeated places where the pencil strokes will cross one another and where the result will be a darkening.

In the end, after hundreds of repetitions, there may be a gray area around the main thrust of his pencil strokes, but the crossings will concentrate along the lines and curves the writer is trying to make. The result will be that his name will appear sharper, darker, and more even than any single pencil stroke could have made it.

If you then imagine the pencil strokes removed one by one, the whole name will still be there, but it will gradually grow dimmer and fuzzier. This is analogous to removing more and more of the pattern repetitions on the hologram by tearing, piercing, scratching, or dusting.

What are the applications of holography? To what use can it be put?

It is not revolutionizing the world all at once, for there is more to technological innovation than the mere working out of a new concept. It has to be made competitive; the concept has to be translated into hardware that will do something not only better than before but more conveniently, more simply, more cheaply, or all three.

For instance, holograms can be made of some structure in double exposure. The object being holographed is left unstressed the first time and is placed under some stress the second. The difference in the interference patterns produced represents defects of one sort or another in specific places in the structure being holographed. In this way holography can be used to test airplane wings, for instance, nondestructively. However, such objects can also be tested by X-rays and ultrasonic sound, and holographic techniques are not sufficiently better or cheaper or more convenient to cause a wholesale shift in nondestructive testing as yet.

Holographic techniques could be used to produce three-dimensional television or movie effects, but holography produces too much information for television or movie techniques to handle just yet. Holography must wait for the older systems to catch up to its advances.

Nevertheless, holography can do some things right now that cannot be done otherwise. One interesting application is its use in deblurring fuzzy photographs. It was the desire to do this that led Gabor to the original invention of the technique with respect to electron microphotographs.

Photographs can be blurred through known failings in the system used. However, a laser beam can be passed through the blurred photograph, and an interference pattern can be produced that will cancel out the effects of the failings. A new photograph appears in which the blurring has been greatly reduced.

The technique has been applied very successfully to the photographs taken by electron microscope. Such deblurring extends the range through which electron microscopes can produce successful magnifications. By use of the technique, the double helix of virus nucleic acid was shown for the first time, and eventually single atoms may be made out.

It is also quite possible that holograms will be employed for the storage of information, a use for which their three-dimensional properties are not needed. For instance, holograms might replace ordinary photographic techniques in many cases, since the holograms would be insensitive to scratching and minor damage that would be sufficient to spoil ordinary photographic film. TV cassettes may therefore become holographic eventually.

Then, too, hundreds of pictures can be recorded holographically on a single piece of film. When laster light is made to shine through the film at a series of angles, each differing slightly from the next, a whole series of different interference patterns is formed with a whole series of different objects. These can then all be projected as a laser beam shines on the completed hologram, first at one angle, then at another. Image after image appears and the *Encyclopaedia Britannica* might be stored on a hologram the size of a sheet of typing paper—a sheet that under ordinary photographic techniques could record but one image and no more. This same ability to store enormous quantities of information may result in the development of holographic memories for computers.

However, it is useless to attempt prediction too closely in order to see what holographic techniques might do, for instance, to aid medical diagnoses or surgical methods. Technology often takes surprising turns. Holography is a versatile means of handling large quantities of information, and exactly how it may be applied could depend on ingenious discoveries that would prove as sudden, as unexpected, and as productive as Gabor's original inspiration proved to be.

Chapter 10

somebody
up there
like me

James Freedman and Henry Korn

In February of 1972, the National Aeronautics and Space Administration launched Pioneer 10, the first man-made object programmed to depart from the confines of our solar system not only for points unknown but perhaps even beyond imagining.

The rocket carries one of the most incredible communiqués in the whole of human history: a 6-by-9-inch gold-anodized plaque engraved with a message designed to communicate to a possible extraterrestrial recipient our cosmic location, epoch, and basic nature by showing a planetary chart, a pulsar map, a hydrogen molecule, and a picture of a man and a woman.

As testament to the effectiveness of the plaque's ability to stimulate communication, it readily succeeded in arousing the curiosity and further involvement of the coauthors of this article. Shortly after the launch, we interviewed one of its designers, Dr. Frank Drake of Cornell University and Director of the National Astronomy and Ionosphere Center in the hopes of gaining an understanding of the project's heady implications by recording the history of how it came to be. The first part of this article outlines that history and is followed by a speculative probe of the project's significance.

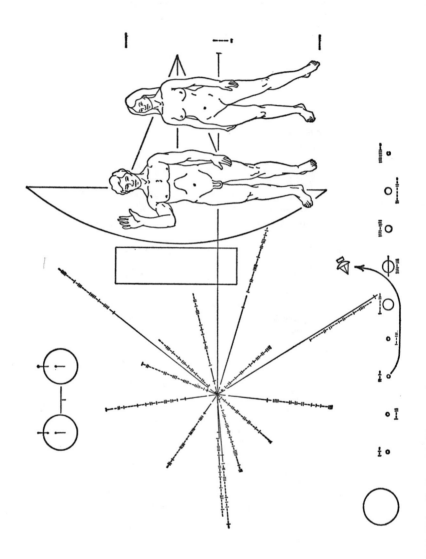

Despite a lifetime devoted, in part, to serious scientific investigation of the possibility of intelligent life on other planets (including a radio astronomy project in which he conducted a systematic search for signals from extraterrestrials), Dr. Drake was given no prior notice from NASA of their ambitious plan to dispatch Pioneer 10 outside the solar system after it completed its probe of the planet Jupiter. Happily, in November of 1971, Drake received word of the plan from a reporter from the *Christian Science Monitor* and was able to swing into action in time for the February launch.

In early December, Drake had an opportunity to share this information with a colleague, Dr. Carl Sagan, coauthor (with Russian scientist I. S. Shklovskii) of *Intelligent Life in the Universe,* an influential study of work in this field from the beginning of recorded history to 1966. Sagan and Drake dispassionately discussed NASA'S plan at a meeting in Puerto Rico. It was quickly agreed that the flight offered a unique opportunity to initiate the first attempt at direct visual communication with the beyond for both the value of the thing itself and to publicize work in this field.

While Drake and Sagan were aware that, if successfully intercepted, the rocket would yield much greater information about its sponsors than the plaque, they also agreed on the value of displaying a conscious attempt to communicate. Thus, they conceived of a plaque that would (1) show the creatures of earth by depicting a man and a woman; (2) impart some basic information on the chemical structure of our world by showing a hydrogen molecule; and (3) attempt to fix our time and galactic location by depicting a map of our solar system and a chart of pulsars known to be emanating from earth by 1972.

On December 8, Dr. Carl Sagan, who had had previous dealings with NASA on the Mariner 9 probe, agreed to approch the agency on behalf of the Pioneer 10 Plaque project. One week later, he telephoned Dr. Drake to report approval for the plan. On December 22, Drake mailed the completed pulsar calculations to Sagan who turned the information over to his artist wife, Lynn Sagan, for final design.

JUST HOW MEDIOCRE WE ARE

Despite occasional bursts of energy and imagination, mankind, like the sun which grants us life, is a distinctly mediocre commodity. We lie together in the mid-outer reaches of one of the spiraling arms of stars that constitute our galaxy. Hot young stars seem to occur along the periphery of the system, farther out on the spiral arms, and the older ones cluster in the more densely populated nucleus. Our sun is neither at the periphery nor the nucleus; it lies somewhere between the outskirts and the center of the galaxy —what some astronomers have called the "suburbs" of the Milky Way.

There are perhaps 150 billion stars in the Milky Way. Of these it is likely that approximately two billion have habitable planets. The physical conditions for terrestrial life, as we know it, are quite common. Earth and its solar system are far from unique— in fact, they are rather typical. The amount of heat given off by our sun in comparison with other stars is neither very high nor very low. Since the mass, distribution, and atmosphere of orbiting bodies are determined in large part by the temperature of their star, the properties of our solar system, like the heat of its sun, are not exceptional. The number of stars that radiate the same approximate amount of heat as our own is very high. And the number of stars that appear to resemble our sun in all aspects, not just heat, is as much as two percent of all stars in the universe.

The conditions for life, using ourselves as a model, are therefore not unique in the universe. Among the numerous variations in galactic systems, we are one of many, many single-star solar systems. Position in the galaxy, proximity to other stars, temperature and age, and most other qualities of our star can not be described as out of the ordinary or extreme. The point is that the conditions of life require no special features—or special concatenation of features—that the universe of possibilities has to offer. The conditions of life are average conditions in most regards. That our star and planet support life can not be considered a "special instance."

TWO PERCENT OF INFINITY

We have said that the minimum estimate for the percentage of stars whose solar systems may have some life is two percent. Is two percent of the universe a lot?

This question poses a dilemma that is concealed by the reserve of most scientists and that unnerves anyone on first considering this subject. Two percent of the universe may seem to be very small when a finite number of things is considered; but it is a lot of infinity. The numbers and figures appear reasonable in one view, but extravagant in another. Any attempt to communicate with extraterrestrial intelligence is at once commendable, urgent, but insanely unreasonable.

Two percent of infinity is enormous. But if we argue—using our average selves as a standard—that the number of life systems occurring around other suns is infinite, we must also argue that the range of variable forms of life is equally infinite. When infinity is a factor, things increase predictably in kind, but increase in form by random and unknown factors.

To assume that our civilization, whose knowledge of radio is only forty years old, should have any basis for communicating with a civilization whose technology might have begun forty million years ago (to use an appropriately arbitrary number) borders on the ridiculous. The possibility of "living" beings existing in the universe is high, but there is not much likelihood they will be like us.

THE MEASURE OF OUR IMPROBABILITY

How fortuitous is the intelligence we possess? The structure of human chromosomes may give us some idea. Chromosomes play the major role during the reproductive process of a cell. They are elongated bodies and contain nucleic acids, DNA and RNA. A DNA molecule is made up of two strands along which are laid out it constituents, called nucleoside phosphates. There are four basic kinds of nucleoside phosphates, and their pattern on the strands governs the reproductive event. As strands of a DNA molecule separate, each seeks in the medium (that is, in its immediate vicinity), the constituents for a new strand; but the new constituents must conform, in the process of combination, to the pattern established by the nucleoside phosphates along the original strand. This keeps the cell from replicating randomly, and assures that we are forever thus and no other.

In the DNA molecule is the genetic code; since it is due to this code that we are reproduced as we are, we may say that the code gives the most concise definition of who we are. There is an extremely large number of positions for nucleoside phosphates. Sagan and Shklovskii have given 4×10^9. In each of the slots, four different combinations are possible. The number of possible varieties of human chromosomes should be, then, *4 to the power of 4 $\times$ 10⁹*. This number, according to Sagan and Shklovskii, is a "measure of our improbability." It is likewise a measure of our fortuity. Since we have said that the structure of the human chromosome is the most appropriate defining feature of our species, we may conclude that there are a lot of things that we might otherwise be.

From one point of view, this number might argue for our admirable evolutionary progress and complexity. More important, however, it indicates the inconceivable diversity that other possible forms of life, even with the same chemistry as ours, might assume. The probability of a form of life and intelligence identical to ours occurring in another galaxy is about as small as two percent of infinity is large.

DETECTING EXTRATERRESTRIAL INTELLIGENCE

Actual contact in the near future with intelligent life in other solar systems proceeds against severe odds, for reasons other than the unlikelihood of mutual comprehensibility. Even if another civilization developed along the same physical and mental lines as us, it is unlikely that it has emerged and evolved according to the same timetable. Furthermore, the likelihood that another civilization should know of our existence is slim. It is our radio emissions more than anything else that make us "visible" to others; and we made our debut into the public world of the universe only forty years ago. In 1960, Frank Drake erected a special receiver to search for signals from extraterrestrials. But only those solar systems less than twenty light years away would have, by now, heard of us and would want intentionally to contact us. There are only fifteen such stars, and there is no guarantee that there is life on any of them.

What, then, is the possibility of receiving the "noise" of another civilization—its equivalent of the radio emissions of the earth—and other unintentional messages that make their way to outer space? We can see that the probability of that is small by looking at the future of communication technology on earth. As our technical competence increases, less wasteful means of sending electromagnetic waves will be devised; it is theoretically possible to prevent any radiation from escaping into space. If this happens within sixty years, the span of years that earth will have been "noisy" is not more than a hundred. And generalizing, the span of time that any planet with a technical evolution like ours will be "noisy" is only one hundred years of its entire existence. Our chances of detecting a nearby civilization going through its hundred years of noise prior to the perfection of more efficient means of sending signals seems very slight.

But perhaps getting in touch with extraterrestrials is not the most important consequence of knowing that they exist.

SPACE AS A MIRROR

As Pioneer 10 speeds toward the outer limits of the solar system bearing a plaque for our neighbors, a greater number of people than ever before see themselves not only as living on earth but living in space. Some critics of the project have protested the inferior role of the female on the plaque. Others have used the issue as the subject of a joke. One cartoon showed a bubbly spaceman telling his buddy that it was not supposed to mean anything—it was a work of art. To assume that other examples of life should share the very human failing of mistaking the content of the plaque for its form is in no way an aspersion on the intelligence of space people. It is a way of seeing ourselves more precisely.

The same is true for the scientist as for the cartoonist: conjecture on extraterrestrial life is in fact a springboard for the study of earth. When astronomers speak of technical civilizations in other solar systems, they are speaking also of the future of technological civilization on earth. Knowing life is "out there" is a fuse for the contemporary imagination.

Let us pose a typical problem. Suppose that a civilization has advanced technically well beyond the "noise" stage and has learned how to avoid wasting electromagnetic radiation, and in the process, has also learned to conserve *all* forms of energy, including that of the sun. What sort of signals may we expect from such a civilization? We solve the problem, of course, by using earth as an example.

First of all, such civilizations will be difficult to contact. They will receive only the messages they have provisions for receiving, and will emit only the small amount of solar radiation that escapes from this shell. Given a reasonable width for the shell, one could estimate the wavelength of this escaping radiation to be approximately ten microns. Freeman Dyson has therefore suggested looking for signals of this wavelength—hence, "infrared stars"—as possible seats of highly advanced civilizations.

OUR LOT IN SPACE

Speculation on this matter raises the disturbing question: Will advanced civilizations be at all eager to enter into contact with others? Do curiosity and the desire for progress continue in an aging advanced society that has solved its problems?

An eminent astronomer and futurist, Sebastian Von Hoerner, has foreseen a number of crises for civilizations like ours; among them, he has included population density, irreconcilability of great political powers, natural aggressiveness leading toward self-destruction, and genetic degeneration. The solution of each of these demands the abandonment of some basic ideals: the ethics of competition, self-propagation, and progress. In short, in order to finally solve those problems that threaten contemporary society, there is but one hope. The notion of stagnation—an eternal present—must become a good and readily accepted reality. Stasis is simply a consequence of surviving the crises that threaten a developing civilization. One of its corollaries must be a disregard for anything that upsets the equilibrium of an unchanging society—including extraterrestrial contact. Inquisitiveness, by necessity, will have died. Thus, we are left with one final question:

Do technological civilizations survive?

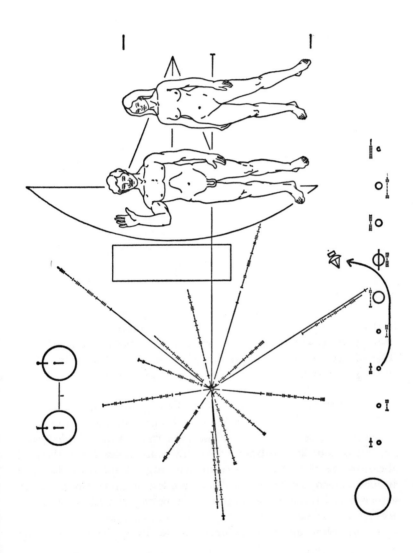

brain power:
the case for
bio-feedback training

Barnard Law Collier

Inside a darkened chamber in the laboratory of Dr. Lester Fehmi sits Ralph Press, a nineteen-year-old mathematics student at the State University of New York in Stony Brook, Long Island. Relaxed in an armchair with his eyes closed, Ralph is undergoing his eleventh session of bio-feedback training to help him learn to control his brain waves.

Four silver electrodes are pasted to Ralph's scalp, their orange lead wires plugged into an electroencephalograph that is tracing his brain-wave activity on thick ribbons of EEG paper in the next room. The silence in the sound-proofed chamber is broken only by the long and short beepings of a rather high-pitched tone: the key to Ralph's bio-feedback training.

Dr. Fehmi, a professor of psychology at Stony Brook, has told Ralph that he can learn to increase his brain's output of an eight-to-fourteen-cycle-per-second brain sine wave called alpha. Alpha waves are one of four known brain waves. They are generated, billions of them, by the tiny electrical pulses that surge through the brain as it does its complex chores. High production of alpha waves is often associated with the objective state of peak mental and physical performance, a relaxed yet extremely sensitive alertness.

Dr. Fehmi and George Sintchak, the Stony Brook psychology

department's chief electronic engineer, have rigged the EEG machine and a computer so that each time Ralph's brain generates a burst of alpha activity the occurrence is recorded, timed, and almost instantly made known to Ralph by means of the beeping tone. The tone is Ralph's bio-feedback. It is an audible signal that lets Ralph be consciously aware of a visceral function, in this case the production of his alpha brain waves, which his mind ordinarily blocks out, ignores, or is unable to perceive without external assistance. When Ralph's brain generates only snippets of alpha radiation, the tone comes in staccato little blips. As he produces more and more alpha, the tone stays on longer and longer. Ralph, of course, wants to succeed by producing as much alpha as he can.

For nearly an hour, Ralph shows minute-by-minute improvement in his ability to keep the tone on. A computer read-out verifies that he is maintaining the tone for a cumulative average of twenty-eight seconds out of each minute. "He's one of our super-subjects," Dr. Fehmi remarks. "He's not the best, but he's getting pretty good."

Ralph's alpha waves are of high amplitude, very rhythmic and regular. This is what they look like as they are traced by the jiggling pens of the EEG machine:

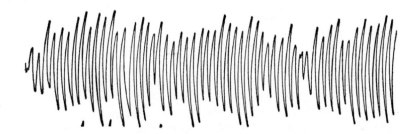

"OK, Ralph," Dr. Fehmi says quietly over the intercom, "I want you to turn the tone off and keep it off."

The tone that Ralph has learned to sustain for upwards of three seconds now goes beep, beep, *blip;* within seconds, it has died away except for tiny random beeps. This is what it looks like on the EEG tracing as Ralph begins to stop his alpha waves:

"Now turn the tone back on," Dr. Fehmi says.

A pause of a second or so and the tone beeps back to life and stays on for seconds at a time. Then on, off, on, off. The tests continue until it is clear that Ralph is in personal command of his brain's alpha-wave activity as evidenced by the EEG machine's record.

A steady flow of new scientific findings indicates that, with the aid of the teaching technique called bio-feedback training, man can learn to control willfully his body and his state of consciousness to a degree that traditionally has been dismissed in Western cultures as mere trickery or condemned as somehow wicked or blasphemous.

Projects in hospitals and research laboratories around the world are convincingly demonstrating that it may be possible to learn personal mastery over the functions of our visceral organs—the heart, liver, kidneys, intestines, glands, and blood vessels—in the same specific way that we learn to manipulate our fingers to play Chopin or our legs to kick a field goal. There is also highly intriguing research going on in laboratories like Dr. Fehmi's to demonstrate that with bio-feedback training we can learn self-control over the electrical activity of our brain. These studies indicate that man may possess the ability to will himself into whatever state of consciousness seems most appropriate to his environment, to accomplishing a task at hand, or to some special pursuit.

The implications of bio-feedback training are proving terribly easy to overstate, given the limited amount of solid experimental evidence that presently exists. People seem peculiarly ready nowadays to lunge at the adventurous prospect of employing new methods and modern technology to explore and conquer one's own brain and body instead of, say, the moon or Southeast Asia. The propensity for exaggeration about progress in this area frightens prudent scientists. Already they are encountering the con artists, the charlatans, and the quacks who are taking people's money by glibly mouthing the jargon associated with bio-feedback research and similar studies of the mind's control over internal organs. This caveat is offered early because it is difficult to keep one's imagination reined in unless one is warned that much of the data accumulated so far are limited to experiments with rats, monkeys, rabbits, or other lab animals. And the remarkable results with animals may not travel well from the laboratory to humans. Nevertheless, research teams are reporting an ever increasing number of cases in which human subjects have unquestionably gained conscious control over visceral organs once thought beyond the mastery of the mind.

In Baltimore, for example, Dr. Bernard T. Engel, a psychologist, and Dr. Eugene Bleecker, a cardiovascular specialist, have conducted bio-feedback training sessions with eight patients suffering from premature ventricular contractions, a dangerous irregularity of the heartbeat involving the heart's main pumping chamber. With significant success, these patients have learned to speed, slow, and narrowly regulate their heart by force of mental discipline alone.

At the Gerontology Research Center of the National Institute of Child Health and Human Development, Dr. Engel and Dr. Bleecker use a visual form of bio-feedback training to help patients control their heart. In a typical experiment, the patient lies quietly on a hospital bed in a small, windowless laboratory near Dr. Engel's office. The electrodes of an electrocardiograph are attached to his chest and pulse points, and the EKG machine is hooked up with a specially programed computer. On the bed table in front of the patient sits a small metal box fitted with a red, a yellow, and a green light in the same pattern as a regular traffic signal. The display is hooked into the computer, which almost instantly analyzes the EKG readings and provides bio-feedback information to the patient by means of the flashing colored lights.

The first phase of the training is speeding the heart rate. The patient may be told that when the yellow light goes on he will know that his heart is beating faster; the green light flashing on means it is slowing down. A small meter next to the light box indicates to the patient what percentage of the time he is succeeding in keeping the yellow light lit. The goal for the heart patient, of course, is to gain control over the lights and his heartbeat in the same way Ralph Press controlled the beeping tone and his alpha-wave production: by sheer mental effort, and without any muscular exertion—which amounts to cheating.

After a patient learns to speed his heart, he is then taught to slow it down with the red light and later to keep it beating within narrow normal limits, with the three lights acting as too fast, too slow, and normal signals. Some of Dr. Engel's patients have achieved a 20 per cent speeding or slowing of their heart—about sixteen beats a minute from an eighty-beat-per-minute base. This self-willed rate change in one direction or the other tends to even out the irregular beats. Why? Researchers are not quite sure, but it works.

But what happens when the patient goes home, away from Dr. Engel's bio-feedback light box? The final stage of the five-phase training program is the stepped withdrawal of the bio-feedback light signals. The patient, after extensive training, finds he can deliberately alter his heartbeats in the desired direction without artificial feedback. One of Dr. Engel's patients could still remember how to control his rate after two years. That Dr. Engel's patients retain what they have learned without the aid of an electronic device to provide feedback is what excites many researchers who feel that we may be capable of discovering unknown mechanisms, or "feedback loops," within ourselves that will allow us, after some basic training, to monitor our viscera and their functions at will throughout life.

In Boston and New York City, scientists are trying to see how people with hypertension can effectively lower their abnormally high blood pressure by thinking it down. Under the direction of Dr. Neal E. Miller, a professor of physiological psychology at Rockefeller University in New York and a pioneer in the brain sciences, experiments are now proceeding to discover if human subjects can learn to control the contractions of their intestinal tract. Laboratory rats have learned to control these contractions with notable success. If humans can do as well, it could mean relief from much suffering for people with spastic colons and similar gastrointestinal ailments usually associated with stress and psychosomatic illness.

Dr. Miller was in the forefront of what seemed, just a decade or so ago, a vain and somewhat foolhardy challenge to the bedrock idea that the viscera and the autonomic nervous system that controls them operate entirely independently of an animal's deliberate control. Dr. Miller has traced back to Plato the dogma that the organs controlled by the autonomic nervous system function at a kind of cave-mannish level, learning only in classical Pavlovian fashion to react to such stimuli as sour lemons and growling bears. On the other hand, the somatic, or cerebrospinal, nervous system, which transmits nerve signals from the brain to the spinal cord and directly to the skeletal muscles, can learn by the sophisticated trial-and-error instrumental process. Perhaps the Greeks considered it an act of hubris to believe that they, not the gods, exercised command of their heart, brain, and guts. Dr. Engel, who also has studied the accumulated prejudices against the viscera, can recite a chain of erroneous proofs put forth until only a few years ago by scientists who, with a kind of religious fervor, had shunned anatomical facts and new information in order to steadfastly support Plato.

At the root of the research reports on bio-feedback training is what Dr. Miller describes as "an almost complete change in our way of thinking about our viscera and their ability to learn. We are now able to regard the activities of our internal organs as behavior in the same sense that the movements of our hands and fingers are behavior. This is the basic stem of it all, but just where this rather radical new orientation will lead, we can't be sure yet."

Some indications that we can possibly control our viscera have been around for centuries without anyone's grasping their import. Dr. Miller points out that actors and actresses can control their tear glands, which are visceral organs, to make themselves cry on cue. It is possible that some classical conditioning is involved: The actor recalls something sad and the sadness makes him cry. But many actors and actresses say they can cry without any recalling, that all they have to do is think "cry" and the tears flow.

Magicians and mystics and meditators have often gained mental control over visceral organs to a significant degree. Harry Houdini is said to have been able to swallow and regurgitate a key that would unlock him from some otherwise unopenable box. If he did this, it would mean he had gained mastery over the muscles of his esophagus and stomach, part of the viscera.

A few yogis, it would seem, can control their metabolism to

some extent. But whether or not they "cheat" by using skeletal muscles instead of only their mind to perform their tricks is unknown. Scientists have found that some yogis who can "stop" their hearts so that no pulse or sound of beating can be detected are actually performing what is called the Valsalva maneuver. By taking a deep breath, closing their windpipe, and breathing hard to increase the pressure inside their chest and around their heart, they collapse the veins to the heart and clamp off the return of blood. This arrests heart sounds and the pulse, but an EKG shows that the heart is still beating and usually quite fast. "We must reexamine a lot of phenomena we may have dismissed as fakery before," Dr. Miller says.

The belief in a "superior" somatic nervous system and an "inferior" automatic nervous system was so strong that, according to Dr. Miller, "for more than a dozen years I had extreme difficulty getting students or even paid assistants to conduct experiments on the control of internal organs." But Dr. Miller persisted, and his research has led many other scientists to abandon the old dogma. He has shown that the internal organs in animals and to a significant extent in man, as well, are capable of learning by trial and error— and with a startling degree of specificity and discrimination. In one experiment, which Dr. Miller particularly enjoys mentioning, he and his research colleague, Dr. Leo V. DiCara, tuned their instrumental conditioning process down so fine that a rat learned to blush one ear and blanch the other. In almost all of his animal experiments, Dr. Miller paralyzes the rats and other lab animals with curare, a powerful drug used by South American Indians to tip their poison darts. The curare interferes with all the nerve impulses that keep the skeletal muscles working—including respiration. The paralyzing of the skeletal muscles ensures that the animals do not "cheat" by somehow using their skeletal muscles to affect their visceral responses. (It is thus far a frustration for Dr. Miller and others that non-curarized animals are slower to learn viscerally than the curarized ones.)

The difference between the way the body learns by classical conditioning and by instrumental conditioning is crucial to understanding how bio-feedback training works. Classical conditioning, or learning, always demands a stimulus that elicits an innate response. For example, the first time you ever saw a lemon, nothing much happened with your saliva glands, which are visceral organs. But after you first tasted its sour juice, your saliva glands automatically secreted lots of saliva to dilute and wash away the puckering citric acid. You cannot control the response of your saliva glands to the lemon juice, and after you have tasted several lemons your mouth will start watering at the very sight of one. You have been classically conditioned to salivate at the sight of lemons. The same thing works for other such stimuli: a mad dog, for example. The sight of one will boost your heart rate, increase your adrenaline flow, and generally activate other innate fear responses.

The process of instrumental learning is much less limited since it requires no specific stimulus to provoke a response. If you want to sink a twelve-foot golf putt, for instance, there is nothing anyone can offer you, not a lemon or $5,000, that will get your body to hole the ball out with Pavlovian sureness. But by the process of trial and error, or instrumental conditioning, you can learn to coordinate your muscles and other responses. You stroke the ball toward the hole and it glides by. You try again and again. Each time you get closer. You are not aware of precisely what you are doing to improve; you cannot say which muscles are contracting or relaxing and in what order. But you get closer nonetheless, and each near success is a reward that is likely to keep you trying. At last you are in control of your muscles, your responses, and the golf ball. It plunks into the hole. This trial-and-error process is called instrumental learning.

Now imagine that you are trying to make the same putt blindfolded. Very difficult, if not impossible. Why? Because something essential is missing from the learning process: feedback. In this case, the feedback is the sight of the ball getting closer to the cup. Of course, you could learn to make the putt blindfolded if you substituted for the feedback of your visual perception the voice (feedback) of your caddy. He might, at the simplest level, say "yes" when your direction was right and say nothing or "no" when it wasn't. He might offer more guidance: "A little more to the right" or "A little to the left and harder." You would still be badly handicapped by the imprecision of your caddy's secondhand information, but eventually you would sink one and then perhaps quite a few.

Our mind is in some ways like the blindfolded golfer where the viscera are concerned. Scientists are trying to find new ways to remove the blindfold, which is enormously difficult indeed, or to substitute the guidance of the caddy-type feedback for sensory information about visceral organs that the mind for some reason dismisses or never perceives. Dr. Fehmi's beeping tone and the minivolt currents of pleasurable brain stimulation that lab rats get are simple reward bio-feedback signals; Dr. Engel's colored lights represent more guidance. All are examples of bio-feedback used to instrumentally condition internal organs by letting the mind know, within predetermined limits, what those organs are up to.

One path of bio-feedback research has branched slightly away from the strictly therapeutic approach and is investigating the ability of human beings to exert purposeful control over their visceral functions, especially their brain functions, with the goal of making the essentially healthy person better able to cope with his world. At the United States Navy Medical Neuropsychiatric Research Unit in San Diego, California, Dr. Ardie Lubin and Dr. David Hord, both psychologists, are studying the relationship between the output of alpha waves and sleep. What they want to determine is whether or not a person deprived of sleep can be returned to a state of effectiveness and acceptable decision-making capacity by willing himself into an alpha state for a certain length of time. Some preliminary tests have shown that alpha states may be recuperative.

At the Langley Porter Neuropsychiatric Institute, part of the University of California Medical Center in San Francisco, a research group headed by Dr. Joe Kamiya is exploring the possibility that brain-wave control may have important effects on health, creativity, and such mental functions as perception and memory. Dr. Kamiya is regarded by most psychologists as the pioneer in the field of brain-wave control. Dr. Kamiya and his research team have found that subjects who do best at mastering their alpha-wave output are those who have had some training in meditation, as in Zen. At Stony Brook, Dr. Fehmi has noted that musicians, athletes, and artists are especially adept at control over their brain waves. Conversely, he has found that subjects who come into his chamber and slouch in their armchair in the spaced-out way associated with drug trips produce precious little alpha.

It is frustrating to researchers that the subjects who are most proficient in gaining brain-wave control are often strangely tongue-tied when it comes to telling just how they do it. Some say they relax and wipe everything from their mind. Others concentrate on some infinite point like a mystical third eye in the middle of their forehead. Some are unable to verbalize the experience at all.

"The best way I can describe the feeling of alpha," says Dr. Fehmi, "is a relaxed but alert and sensitive 'into-it-ness.' " Dr. Edgar E. Coons, a physiological psychologist at New York University and a musician, has been trained to produce alpha waves in Dr. Fehmi's lab; he says the alpha state "makes me feel as if I'm floating about half an inch above my seat." A talented young musician named David Rosenboom, who recently presented a bio-feedback brain-wave concert at Automation House in New York (brain-wave activity was fed into a computer and an ARP synthesizer; the result was a weird but not unpleasing effect), is the reigning champion brain-wave producer for Dr. Fehmi. When his alpha is really going strong in all parts of his brain, Rosenboom says he is plugged in to a "great energy source." Another musician named LaMonte Young, who keeps a forty-cycle "home" tone going in his Manhattan studio at all times, explained that he had no trouble generating alpha the first time he ever tried it, because his mind "is tuned to frequencies and intervals."

At the University of Colorado Medical School, Dr. Hans Stoyva has had notable success in teaching his patients how to relax specific muscles that tense up and cause certain kinds of tension headaches. The easing of pain has been swift and dramatic.

Dr. Martin Orme, director of experimental psychiatry at the University of Pennsylvania Medical School in Philadelphia, is studying the alpha-wave phenomenon with an eye toward finding out what exactly an alpha state does to or for an individual and how it might be beneficial to him. "It's not enough to know you can contemplate your navel," Dr. Orme says. "You then have to ask, 'What happens?' " Experiments conducted with subjects who have been trained to produce a reliably high alpha-wave output show, according to Dr. Orme, that critical thinking tends to interfere with alpha waves, but that alpha-wave production does not mean blunted intellectual capacity. What alpha production seems to do best for the alpha producer is relax him, insulate him from stressful critical thought, and rehabilitate his autonomic nervous system to some degree.

"What this may mean," Dr. Orme says, "is that alpha might be used to bring down the level of a person's anxiety to a point where he can function at his best. We all need a certain amount of anxiety to function. It is well accepted that we function best as anxiety rises to a certain point on a bell-shaped curve, and past that point we do increasingly worse as anxiety increases. If alpha can be used to knock down anxiety to the point on the curve where we work most effectively, it can be a most important development." However, Dr. Orme is quick to point out that "this is three levels or more from where we are now, but it is something to consider."

Another prospect for visceral learning is its use as a possible alternative to drugs. If, for example, a high alpha output can cause deep relaxation, or a specific focusing of bio-feedback training can loosen up a taut muscle, this could well substitute for the billions of tranquilizers consumed to achieve essentially the same effect. The advantage over drugs might be considerable. For instance, while a tranquilizer acts in a general way on the whole body or an entire bodily system (perhaps with unwanted side effects), bio-feedback training might be specific enough to do the job required and let the rest of the body function undisturbed.

"There is also," says Dr. Orme, "the general question of personal control and how we might be able to bring our emotions under control. We want to know, of course, to what extent an individual can gain control with precision and reliability over the things he fears. A good part of fear is the fear of fear. If you know you are going to be hurt, you will hurt more with exactly the same degree of hurting stimulus. If we can break into some of the feedback loops that are part of the fear cycle, we may be able to control unpleasant and unproductive anxiety."

To Dr. Orme, the goal is clear. "We may be able to become actual masters of our destiny. As a psychiatrist, my purpose is to enable man to decide his own fate instead of his juices deciding for him."

At Rockefeller University, Dr. DiCara, a burly ex-football player, is attempting to unravel some of the whys and hows of visceral learning. In one recent experiment, he and Dr. Eric Stone found that rats trained to increase their heart rate had significantly more of a powerful group of chemicals called catecholamines in their brains and hearts than rats who learned to *lower* their heart rates. In humans, catecholamines are associated with hypertension and coronary artery disease. The possibility of learning to slow the heart rate to achieve beneficial effects on hypertension and heart ailments is intriguing; however, a major obstacle still to be overcome is the inability at present to measure catecholamines in the human brain.

An equally intriguing possibility has been raised by an experiment conducted by Dr. DiCara and Dr. Jay M. Weiss. Rats that had learned to slow their heart rates subsequently showed excellent ability to learn to move back and forth in a shuttle box to avoid an electric shock. Rats trained to speed their hearts learned very poorly and exhibited signs of extreme fearfulness by leaping into the air, squealing, and turning toward their tails with each pulse of shock instead of getting away from it. In contrast, the slow heart-rate rats took each shock in stride, with only "mild jerks," and slowly walked out of the electrified side of the box.

"It is crystal-clear," says Dr. Miller, with whom Dr. DiCara has worked as co-experimenter on many projects, "that heart rate training affects rats' learning. What is further indicated is that the training also affects their emotionality. We cannot jump from the laboratory to the clinic, but we may indeed find that in human subjects trained to lower their heart rates there could be an increased capacity to adapt to stressful situations and a corresponding decrease in emotionality."

The field of bio-feedback training and visceral learning is still only crudely charted. New research teams are forming to explore further; the mechanical and electronic spin-offs of the space age are providing the new tools and infinitely more sensitive measuring devices that are required for progress. But most of all there seems to be a new attitude.

"We have brought four to five thousand years of cultural myths into the laboratory to be investigated," says Dr. Miller, who, in just a few years, has seen the pendulum of interest swing from "great resistance to great readiness." Although he is understandably reluctant to speculate on what the future holds, he is nonetheless confident that the new knowledge about our internal organs will stimulate much more research into the astonishing ability of human beings to learn.

the impact of
the new media

Discussions of the impact of the new media are necessarily speculative. Since most of the new media have yet to find widespread application, the consequences of their use cannot be known. Many of the new media have not been fully developed and it can be anticipated that with their technological sophistication will come many presently unpredictable impacts. Thus, discussion of their impact falls within the domain of that special way of thinking we call futurology. As it is true that fifty years ago our world could not have been accurately predicted it is certain that any description of what the world will be like under the influence of the new media is merely conjecture.

Nevertheless, if the question of impact is difficult to approach precisely, it is still worth our consideration. The essays that follow were chosen because of the implications of the new media they illuminate. Each points the way toward several fundamental changes the new media will help to bring about.

The new media will change perceptions, and changed perceptions lead to changed lives. I have included my essay "Lewis—The Electronic Person" as one example of the many accounts of human beings who have developed new lifestyles and life orientations of greater compatibility with the age that lies before us than with our own. As the new media become the customary media of young people generational differences will increase in scope and magnitude. The electronic environment, cybernetic thinking, and perceptions formed by involvement with the new media will foster the growth of human beings whose lives are fundamentally unlike those lives which preceded them. My essay is a personal account of what I think will become a widespread phenomenon.

Few are as capable of describing the full range of new perceptions as is John Lilly. A pioneer of the cybernetic consciousness, Lilly has innovated many ways of applying what we know about systems to human and other life forms. Here the mysterious loses little of its wonder and gains a vocabulary and a way of thinking that brings those things believed to be incomprehensible into rational purview. Eventually as we learn from the new media we will translate new information into anthrocentric data. Lilly has begun the process. Paul Pietsch's essay is yet another insight into our own behavior. Pietsch's translation of holographic theory into a theory of the human mind points the way to one of the most, if not *the* most exciting avenues for future discovery: neurobiology.

Still many readers may find insight into the human mind of little importance to the conduct of day-to-day life experience. Peter Goldmark is the father of videotape and the holder of many of the major new media patents. His essay is a substantive account of the ways he feels the new media will affect current life/work styles. Though speculative, many of Goldmark's postulations appear to be quite reasonable, and we can be fairly certain that as the new media's impact is felt throughout society we will not continue to "conduct business as usual."

Though these essays do point to certain areas where impact is certain to be experienced they scratch the surface and only point to the overwhelming possibilities of transformation resulting from the new media.

Speculation of their impact is one way of trying to imagine a world that will be different from our own sooner than ours became unlike late nineteenth century America. Within certain fields like medicine, education and psychiatry the impact of the new media will be incalculable. As I have tried to indicate in earlier sections the question that faces us is, How much of the future impact of the new media will be guided by reasonable and humane decision, and how much will be the result of the reckless assertion of the social and cultural narrowness so pervasive in the present environment. At the heart of the question of impact, then, is the present conflict of values. What we do or do not do today is a choice designing tomorrow.

Chapter 12

lewis —

the electronic

person

Barry Schwartz

I met Lewis in June, 1971, at a time when the tired critics were
trying hard to drum up new labels for the 1970s. They were not
succeeding. The politics of protest seemed to have spent itself in
grieving. The *New York Times* pictured beer halls and football
stadiums, complete with raccoon coats. *The Greening of America*
seemed as removed from June of 1971 as did Kenneth Kenniston's
Young Radicals from his book four years before, entitled *The Un-
committed.*

Elvis Presley had come back, while everyone sat in the dol-
drums of a social stasis. Jesus Freaks were trying hard to make us
believe something was happening, but somehow the media men
were not able to go far on religious fanaticism. Tim Leary had
been excommunicated and was in exile; Eldridge Cleaver was
thawing out in the North African sun. The songs of the 1950s returned, and company vice-presidents of the 1950s were now assuming the chairmanships. The war in Vietnam continued, but nearly
everyone acted as if it had passed; the counterculture had passed,
and nearly everyone acted as if it were still here. It was not a de-
pressing time; it was a waiting time.

The first impression I had of Lewis was that, amidst the social
lethargy of 1971, he could not stop moving. His legs leaped to the
tune of some personal Olympics, his mouth made noises, his hands

drummed to the lead of some unknown guitar as he beat them against the sides of chairs. It was all very striking; Lewis had an energy I had not really seen before.

It would be easy to attribute the ritualistic motions of this twenty-year-old to random eroticism, hypertension, nonspecific neurotic behavior. Our first conversations confirmed my feeling that I did not understand Lewis. And since I like to feel I understand things, I knew that I could only enter into a relationship with him if I understood that I did not understand him. With his help I would come to know what Lewis was about.

Although Lewis and I shared much in common, held many of the same views on the world and on the trivial, and enjoyed many of the same activities, I found that our similar qualities had evolved in radically different ways. When I heard myself talking, I realized how much of what I know, my range of intellectual understanding, my background information, all derived from a very restricted and highly definable method of inquiry—print. Throughout our discussions I referred to things, ideas, persons, allusions, and metaphors known from literary experience; and my logic smiled when it flowed and frowned when it was required to question its own premises. In contrast to Lewis, I was a cognitive man. Though Lewis and I ultimately shared many philosophic, social, and cutural values, it was not by cognitive units and print logic that Lewis had achieved his brilliance.

Lewis was, in flesh and bone, what Marshall McLuhan and others said he would be. He was not literary, not particularly logical; he did not read, perhaps could not read, and many of his pronouncements were offered as one-liners, lacking full development, careful articulation, and the smooth logic that enabled me to consider my views as conclusions. Lewis's world view emanated from the lifelong experiences he had had with mind-expanding drugs, music, and electricity. Where I would say, "I remember when reading Sartre that . . . ," he would say, "It was when I was tripping at Steve's. . . ." Our conclusions might be the same, often identical, but the building blocks and the very foundation of our experience upon which our insights were based were fundamentally unalike.

I learned a great deal about the loss of absolutes, the relativity of experience, and the inconsequential nature of life itself by reading about it; Lewis learned about it by sensory declassification, experiences of time warp, and the entire range of philosophic insights to be had when, under the influence of LSD or sensory overload, he experienced his death and his rebirth innumerable times. Throughout our conversations we came to realize that our communication would not be satisfactory unless we stopped evaluating our methods and started sharing our conclusions.

Lewis's primary modes of learning were experienced as "trips." The word is helpful here because it suggests moving and changing, and in many ways this was one key to Lewis's value system. That which did not move, flow, or change was stagnating. We shared a deep dislike and distrust of "boredom." But for me boredom was intellectual, cognitive, and communicative stasis. Lewis experienced boredom as not moving, being held, being prevented from changing and behaving spontaneously. Though our responses to boredom were remarkably the same, our experience of it differed. Lewis experienced a time phenomenon where I experienced a flow phenomenon. Boredom was, in Lewis's mind, an abyss into which one fell, for he experienced time with enormous intensity. Boredom, in my terms, was a detour on a linear track. He defined boredom as sensory deprivation; I experienced boredom as intellectual dullness.

Other differences emerged. Lewis had no difficulty doing many things at the same time. He was always reacting to several experiences simultaneously. When I was doing something, an additional activity was perceived as a distraction. He would speak to me for hours, all the time listening intently to the pounding melodic rhythms of his favorite rock groups. Initially, at such times, I felt as if I could not hear myself think. He said it was not important to hear myself think; it was only important to think.

Lewis had a very simplistic view of the world: them and us; new consciousness and old. I had a very complex view of the world; there were many facets to consider, great intricacies, levels of contradiction and confusion, nuances that might escape my attention. If Lewis was a nit, I was a nit-picker.

While listening to music, Lewis would touch controls that altered the ranges of sound imperceptively, and having done so, he would radiate satisfaction. I could hear no difference. His car was wired like a sound studio. His home was full of buttons and dials. Above his bed hung a color television set, and on it he watched the videotapes he made. On each side of the bed were enormous Altec Lansing speakers, the kind used in motion-picture houses. His work with videotape consisted mostly of original designs for sensory dislocation and highly innovative concepts for the creation of experiences. His fascinations with ideas that seemed to have no possible application, his unrealistic expectations of future events, his electronic disgust with the mechanical world were the chief features that separated us.

He did not, as one might expect, function well within the "straight" world, not nearly as well as I. But then again, he had less need to do so, for the world could offer him little more than the money he needed to fund his latest research project. He had no need for status, social approval, or a career. Though his relationship to the outside world would create enormous practical problems for him, perhaps even eventually defeat him, his was not a psychic problem, only a material one. Lewis had made up his mind about the world; his confusions arose only from the difficulties of implementing his strategies. He complained that he had to waste a lot of time.

But beyond his search for resources, the world he wished to live in was at home. Each day was spent inventing, coercing far-fetched ideas into workable schemes, and relating to those who were already of his world. His interests ranged from sensory feedback devices, to nuclear engines, to human flying machines, to expounding the view that modern communication systems destroy the concept of the city. Whenever the pressure was on him, he sat near the AC plug.

Lewis was raised on electronic and psychedelic experiences. Surrounded by the middle-class values of his parents, he learned the relativity of all values, the insubstantiality of possessions, and the positive consequences of egolessness. While his parents talked of security, every night under the influence of some new media he experienced continual change. He does not read, partly by choice and partly, because of his time referencing, by necessity. He accepts his limitations while maintaining a view of himself as always changing, always capable of reincarnation. He feels he is an early forerunner of a new man, a result of voluntary evolution, born too early to be part of a community, born too late to submit to the mentality of the mechanical world. With others like him, he hopes to create pockets of electronic sanity. Though he is bitter when evaluating young people generally, he is basically optimistic and is propelled by his own ability to get inside himself.

Though he is exceptional in the sense that he has had to compromise less than many, and has been less scarred by the encounter with old values, I believe that he is only a more substantial version of a sensibility found among many others who share his orientation, values, and perceptions.

I am not sure what it all means, and I suspect Lewis and I will know each other a very long time, partly in order to find out. Certainly we have influenced each other enormously. I think that I have made it possible for him to know more, and consequently to do more, and that he has done the same for me. If the print culture and the electronic environment are incompatible, they are so only in the extreme. Lewis and I were able to mesh the best of both worlds by incorporating aspects of each other's experience. In the end we were able to communicate, grow, and change together.

I think that I am more capable than Lewis of living in the present and that he is more prepared to experience the future. The media that taught him are new, and because they are new, he lives with a sense of discovery and immediacy. The media that are mine, and will always be mine, are not new and may soon be exhausted and unable to grow. If this is the case, they may tell us more about what has been and even what is; and yet, they may be increasingly unable to communicate what will be.

Lewis and I have lent our media to each other. How much we have mutually incorporated them will be known only in time, and that, at least at this moment, is the only thing we can be certain we will have.

Chapter 13

from dolphins
to lsd: a conversation
with john lilly

Sam Keen

SAM KEEN: If there is a cartographer of altered states of conscious-ness—of the highways and byways of the inner trip—it is John Lilly. You are indeed a rare combination of scientist and mystic. You have traveled from the natural sciences to the esoteric sciences. You seem to incarnate the dissatisfaction that many moderns feel with the narrowly scientific way of knowing and being in the world. But many people still think of you first as the man who communicates with dolphins, so perhaps this is a good place to begin your story. How did you get into dolphin research?

JOHN LILLY: There were several motivating interests. I had been working in brain and mind research for many years. In 1954 I began work in physical isolation in a water-filled tank. While floating around in the tank I began to wonder about the mind of an animal who lived in water all the time and had a brain the size of man's. I knew the dolphin had a cerebral cortex as large as a human's. What was going on in that brain? Some people argued that a large body required a large brain. But there was the example of the whale shark who weighed 40 tons and had a brain the size of a macaque monkey. So I began to ask: what is the dolphin doing with all that excess brain? When I began to study dolphin sounds I found they had an immensely more complex communication system than we do. This led me to question whether we might establish interspecies communication. If this could be done it would show us what the human mind has in common with other creatures with large brains. This knowledge, in turn, might prove valuable if our space program should detect nonhuman, intelligent beings outside the earth.

KEEN: What were the major problems you faced in communicating with dolphins?

LILLY: The first problem was attitude. The human species is so arrogant it is difficult for us to entertain the idea that there may be superior beings swimming around in the sea. So we had to approach the dolphins with gentleness and respect and with the assumption that they had as much desire to communicate with us as we did with them.

Then there was the problem of the different structure of dolphin and human languages. Our vocal communication is airborne and is relatively slow. The dolphin sonic communication is waterborne and is thus about ten times faster than ours. This means the dolphin receives the bulk of his information about his environment acoustically while we receive ours visually. The visual inputs in the dolphin are only one tenth the capacity of our visual inputs, but their acoustical inputs are ten times greater than ours. So the total amount of information received by dolphins and humans from their environments is roughly the same. But the types differ. We are not going to understand dolphins adequately until we can translate their language to ours. We need to experience how they hear their world.

KEEN: How did you establish communication with them?

LILLY: It began with an accident. One day in 1955 we were listening to a tape of dolphin sounds. We suddenly got the weird feeling that the dolphins were mimicking our speech. In fact, they were laughing at us. So, someone suggested that we go out and see if one of our young dolphins, Elvar, would copy a word. We went into the tank and I shouted at Elvar "water." He came up, put his blowhole in the air and went "wa . . . ter," breaking the word in the middle. And so we started to work on the word *water* and within twenty minutes Elvar was copying it.

Later we set up a more intensive experiment in which a young woman, Margaret Howe, lived with and became teacher, friend, mother and lover to a young male dolphin by the name of Peter.

She taught him to reproduce simple words with humanoid sounds, to respond to greetings, to distinguish objects, to say the names of numbered balls, and to respond to elaborate directions. In time they developed genuine verbal and nonverbal communication. Margaret Howe would say "Peter, go get the orange ball." There might be five balls all of different colors floating on the water. Peter would go and bring back the blue ball, the green ball, etc. Every one but the orange ball. An operant conditioner observing Peter might conclude that he didn't understand what we were saying. But Margaret would say "He knows damn well what I mean because he brought me the orange ball five times in a row yesterday on command."

KEEN: If you can break the rules in a creative way it means you must understand the rules.

LILLY: Right. A pigeon might peck the right button five times but a dolphin won't. He is too smart and having too much fun. He changes the rules of the game because he is intelligent enough to get bored with over-simple games. He is trying to get a message across to you. You just can't do the operant-conditioning game with someone who is really intelligent and insists on having a good time. If you want to examine the intelligence of a superior being you have to be willing to observe him on his terms.

KEEN: Some critics suggest that neutral researchers cannot replicate your results. How do you answer this?

LILLY: The basic question at issue here is the status of the scientific observer: who is watching what under what conditions with what assumptions? If we are going to test the hypothesis that dolphins have intelligence equal to or superior to human beings, we have to be willing to adopt the perspective of the dolphins. Treat a dolphin like a stupid animal and that is all you will observe. The operant conditioner is sitting back as an omniscient observer judging the animal and expecting certain reproducible behavior. If he doesn't get that behavior he considers the animal stupid. He doesn't think to ask a new question, as one does with an intelligent human.

KEEN: A scientific observer must be willing to be changed by the object he is investigating.

LILLY: Yes. There is always continuous feedback between the observer and the system he is observing. The observer must always simultaneously be building a model of the system he is observing and of the observer. John van Neuman and Leo Szilard showed this for quantum mechanics. To do quantum mechanics correctly you have to have the quantum observer who goes down into the system to be observed and he has to follow certain laws of observation depending on the system. When he comes back into the Newtonian universe with its large assemblages of matter he must become a Newtonian observer. And when he goes up near the velocity of light he has to become an Einsteinian observer. So, when you start observing dolphins you have to become a dolphin observer. A dolphin observer is not, by definition, an operant conditioner. He must be sensitive, respectful and involved with his (hypothetically) superior animals in an ethical way.

KEEN: Why did you stop working with dolphins?

LILLY: In 1964 I built an eight-foot tank, filled it with sea water and began my work with LSD and physical isolation. The dolphins were in the same lab and I began to see the ethical implications of my beliefs about dolphins. If what I believed about dolphins was true I had no right to hold them in a concentration camp for my scientific convenience. So I decided to end the project. On the day I arrived at this decision, but before I had told any of my colleagues, my favorite dolphin decided to commit suicide.

KEEN: How does a dolphin commit suicide?

LILLY: Sissy just stopped eating. We gave her animal enzymes to stimulate her appetite and got her going for a while. But she finally decided to hell with it and stopped breathing. We had her for seven years, since she was nine months old, and she liked us better than she liked dolphins. After this, five more dolphins committed suicide within two weeks. So I told everyone about my decision and we turned the three remaining dolphins loose.

KEEN: Do you intend to do any further research with dolphins?

LILLY: If I could get the right conditions. I would have to have a wet house by the sea designed so the dolphins could come and go at will. Then I would like to have a family with young children that could learn to play and communicate with young dolphins. I think only such a long-range, free project will allow us to take the next step in interspecies communication.

KEEN: I would like to go back to your research on the effects of LSD and physical isolation. Was this connected with your dolphin work?

LILLY: No. I began the experiments with physical isolation when I was with NIMH in Washington. In neurophysiology there has long been a question of what keeps the brain going. Where are its energy sources? One obvious answer was that the energy sources are strictly biological and internal and they do not depend on the outside environment. But some people were arguing that if you cut off all the stimuli to the brain it would go to sleep. So we decided to test this hypothesis. This was easily done by creating an environment in a tank that would isolate a person from external stimuli. For a couple of years I periodically immersed myself in the tank and studied my states of consciousness. During this time I did not use LSD. Many of my colleagues at NIMH were working with it but I did not want to prejudice my observations about the psychedelic spaces I was getting into in the tank.

KEEN: What happens to your body when you are in a stimulus-free environment?

LILLY: You can forget your body and concentrate on the workings of your mind. But if any stimulus remains it becomes overwhelming. Once when I was in the tank a series of bubbles formed from the water and began to hit my foot. As each bubble traveled up my leg I experienced an exquisite pleasure. In fact, the pleasure was so great that it turned to pain when the bubbles began to come at about five-second intervals.

KEEN: Were the effects of physical isolation comparable to those you later discovered in using LSD?

LILLY: The effects are similar. It is possible in the tank for the person who knows how to relax, to *park his body,* to go into any of the psychedelic spaces without using LSD. Only the energy level differs. LSD allows you to jack the energy level way up. Physical, mental and spiritual energy runs higher.

KEEN: It is difficult to believe that physical isolation produces such dramatic changes. Do you need elaborate training or a special facility to get to psychedelic levels of consciousness without drugs?

LILLY: Certainly it is easier to reach a level of consciousness or a psychic space once you have been there before. But all the average person has to do is to get into the tank in the darkness and silence and float around until he realizes he is programming everything that is happening inside his head. You are free of the physical world at that point and anything can happen inside your head because everything is governed by the laws of thought rather than the laws of the external world. So you can go to the limits of your conceptions.

KEEN: Your imagination is totally free?

LILLY: Well, I don't like the word "imagination." When you are in the tank you are certain of the reality of what you are experiencing. I started off with the notion that I was creating everything I experienced. But a lot of things happened that made me ask some radical questions about the nature of reality and different modes of perception. I began then to see that interpreting all the novel experiences in the tank as projections was an arrogant assumption.

KEEN: What kinds of experiences did you find difficult to interpret in common-sense terms?

LILLY: I went through an experience in which another person I knew apparently joined me in the dark, silent environment of the tank. I could actually see, feel and hear her. At other times I apparently tuned in on networks of communication from other civilizations in other galaxies. I experienced *parking* my body and traveling to different places.

KEEN: This could well sound like a report from a first-class schizophrenic. What kept you from interpreting these experiences as evidence of psychosis?

LILLY: I think the attempt to define all mystical, transcendental and ecstatic experiences which do not fit in with the categories of consensus reality as *psychotic* is conceptually limiting and comes from a timidity which is not seemly for the honest, openminded explorer. Also, I knew something about the world of psychotics. I had a complete training analysis with Robert Walder and had a speaking acquaintance with my own psychotic spaces, and I had worked with catatonic and schizophrenic patients. It was not psychosis I was exploring in the tank but belief structures. I was examining the way in which we program our beliefs and impose limits on what we may perceive and experience by these beliefs. I wanted to know what principles were governing the human mind. If we consider the human mind as a kind of computer, I was looking for the basic programs which were built into the computer and the meta-programs which we impose upon the mind by conscious choice or unconscious compulsion. And I wanted to discover how many of the meta-programs could be raised to the conscious level and be changed, or reprogrammed.

KEEN: Did you discover any essential rules that can serve as guides to the explorer of inner space?

LILLY: After ten years in the tank I formulated a working rule: whatever one believes to be true either is true or becomes true in one's own mind, within limits to be determined experimentally and experientially. These limits themselves are, in turn, beliefs to be transcended. The limits of one's beliefs set the boundaries for possible experience. So every time you reach a limiting belief it must be examined and gone beyond. For the explorer there are no final *true* beliefs.

Compulsion is being trapped in a *known* psychic reality, a dead-end space. Freedom is in the unknown. If you believe there is an unknown everywhere, in your own body, in your relationships with other people, in political institutions, in the universe, then you have maximum freedom. If you can examine old beliefs and realize they are limits to be overcome and can also realize you don't have to have a belief about something you don't yet know anything about, you are free.

KEEN: Did you develop specific techniques in the tank for examining your limiting beliefs?

LILLY: Yes. I have just written a book, *The Center of the Cyclone,* that deals with the rules for exploring the inner-outer spaces of consciousness. The basic skill is one that has been known since ancient times. In yoga and in Eastern thought it has been called establishing the fair witness or the witnessing self. I think of it as becoming an observer and watching the operation of the programs which are governing your thinking and behavior. You can pull out of an experience, step back, and watch the program. Much of psychoanalysis involves gaining this skill of seeing how you have gotten trapped in the past with some program that solved a problem in childhood but that was overgeneralized and carried forward and has continued to operate in inappropriate situations. Tremendous energy is locked up in these old programs or what Jung called "autonomous complexes." You can release this energy if you get enough distance from your emotional involvement in the programs to see them like an old movie on T.V. or like a tape loop that you have heard a thousand times. As soon as you get distance you realize you are not the programmer and you are not that which is programmed and you are not the program. Your identity becomes established as an independent agent. Once this ability to disidentify yourself from old programs, from programming, and from the programmer becomes generalized you have the key to higher states of consciousness. By refusing to identify with the programs you transcend them and gain a measure of control. In this way you begin to exercise the meta-programming powers of the human bio-computer, the ability to create self-consciously the principles that govern thought and behavior.

KEEN: Does the fair-witness technique work for dealing with present experience and future expectations as well as for examining compulsive patterns we have carried over from the past?

LILLY: Of course. Premature judgment and closure is the greatest danger for the person who wants to retain the psychic mobility of the explorer. A good general rule for dealing with situations where you are overwhelmed with novelty is: when you are in a new space where you can't account for what is happening on the basis of past assumptions, stay wide open and let your fair witness store all the information you receive. Later on you can slow down and play it all back without editing and can evaluate what has happened to you.

It is at least an ideal aim to be free of unexamined programs which govern thought and behavior. In Eastern thought this was what was meant by being free of karma. The fair witness is able to function without the imposition of limiting patterns from past experience. I have sometimes described this as the goal of making the human bio-computer general purpose. In this sense I mean that in the general-purpose computer there can be no display, no acting, no ideal that is unavailable to consciousness. This is also near to what Freud meant by the aim of making the unconscious conscious. There should be no boundaries within the computer.

KEEN: You describe continuous iconoclasm that is intoxicating and frightening. I can smell the wind blowing across the vast open spaces but I am not certain it is possible to live in an attitude of continuous exploration. Every time a system of beliefs breaks down or is transcended, the result is chaos and anxiety. Social and psychological limits and boundaries are erected to keep chaos and anxiety within tolerable quantities.

LILLY: No! This is a perfect example of what we have been talking about. And once you recognize it you don't have to follow it. You don't have to suffer continual chaos in order to grow. That is the old Christian program—you can't have heaven without hell, you can't have a cosmos without chaos. This is what I call the trampoline effect.

KEEN: You seem to be challenging one of the more deeply held principles of identity that has governed the Western psyche. I think of Dostoevsky's vision: man knows the angel in himself only to the extent that he converses with his devil. Or of Freud's notion that ego is strong only to the degree that it has integrated the underworld of the id. There is no ascension into heaven without a descent into hell, no resurrection without crucifixion, no success without failure, etc. This rhythm, or oscillation, has been central to the Western notion of growth.

LILLY: I am not denying the existence of a duality, or plurality, in man. I only say that simultaneity rather than oscillation is a better, more economical way of dealing with this duality. You don't have to keep going down in order to go up.

Once you know any "negative" system such as fear exists you can get the energy out of it by rising above it through meditation and observation.

KEEN: There is a growing interest here in psychological disciplines and philosophy of the East. Meditation and yoga are almost as common today as prayer meetings were a generation ago. How did you get into mysticism?

LILLY: I left the Catholic Church when I was 13, when I decided that the whole mystical thing—God, angels, afterlife—was all childish nonsense. I went full speed into science. But when I began my work with physical isolation, I began to experience a super-self level, a network of inter-related essences. Your essence, my essence, everybody's essence is hooked together. And there is immediate and total communication with them all the time throughout the whole galaxy.

KEEN: Is this your way of rendering the experience out of which the classical notion grew that man is a microcosm of the macrocosm, that his reason or logos partakes of the reason or logos that informs all of reality?

LILLY: Yes. But that classical idea never made any sense to me until I experienced the network of intelligences, the galactic or universal network or what was called Universal Mind in Idealistic philosophy and Eastern religion.

In 1964, as the result of an accident, I went through a death experience. I was in a coma for twenty-four hours and was blind for two days after that. In the coma I entered a space I hadn't been in since I was twenty-two, when I had four wisdom teeth pulled under gas. I had also been in the same space at age seven when my tonsils were taken out and when I was five and had t.b. Each time I had almost died, or thought I was going to die. Two characters or guides kept turning up. Every time I have a job to do, these characters show up and tell me what the job is.

In the tank in the Virgin Islands I tried to get back to the place where I had met the guides by using LSD without the fear of death. In spite of some fear, I relaxed, as I was immediately in their space. The two guides began to come toward me from a vast distance. As they approached their presences became powerful and I noticed their thinking, feeling and knowledge pouring into me. Just as I felt I would be overwhelmed by their presence, they stopped. As they stopped, in effect they said, "We will not approach any closer as this seems to be your limit at this time. You can come back here any time once you have learned the routes. We are sent to instruct you. So far you have been doing your experiments in solitude and have learned some of the ways to get here. Now you should contact others like yourself who have these capacities, help them, and learn from them. Perfect your means of communicating with this level but stay in your body. There are other methods than LSD plus solitude for achieving these results."

After these initial contacts I began to feel the presence of my guides without going into their spaces.

KEEN: Does it now seem to you that these guides are more than poetic projections of your own imagination?

LILLY: The two guides may be aspects of my own functioning at the super-self level. They may be helpful constructs, or concepts. They may be representatives of an esoteric hidden school. They may be members of a civilization a hundred, a thousand years or so, ahead of ours. Or I may be tuning in on networks of communication of a civilization beyond ours which is radiating information throughout the galaxy. I don't know.

KEEN: Much of your work with physical isolation and LSD seems to be an effort to establish a set of disciplines for dealing with kinds of experiences which a scientistic culture has considered paranormal or even abnormal. Are we now developing practices that will allow us some orderly access to altered states of consciousness?

LILLY: We are approaching a marriage between the modern scientific point of view and the old esoteric and mystical knowledge. Now we are exploring new modes of access to states of consciousness which have been experienced for centuries. It is an empirical approach to those dimensions of consciousness that Eastern thinkers spoke of as levels of enlightenment or satori. I want to elaborate a series of maps and some rules of the road.

KEEN: What kinds of maps have you developed for the outer spaces of human consciousness?

LILLY: The most helpful one for me was developed by Oscar Ichazo, the master who runs the school in Chile in which I have spent the last eight months. He uses the analogy of the length and frequency of sound waves to characterize the different levels of consciousness. Level 48 is the rational, neutral state. At this level your mind is operating efficiently but without emotion. This is the type of consciousness in which the head tripper lives most of the time. The experiences of different types of satori, or enlightenment, begin at level 24. Level 24 involves enjoyment in doing some activity that is done well and without conflict. This is the professional satori, the state of integrated work. As we move up in the psychedelic scale to level 12 we reach a state of blissful awareness. At level 12 you can't function smoothly in the world because you are in bliss. You still are in your body but the reality around you seems alive. This is the first level of a good LSD trip. At this level it is frequently difficult to speak. You accept the here and now. Sometimes this state can be reached in sexual intercourse. It is also the kind of enlightenment Zen speaks about. At level six you get out of your body for the first time. You become a point of consciousness, love, energy, warmth, cognition. This point is mobile. It can travel inside your body or into outer spaces. You still have your own I, your center of consciousness, but your body is not experienced.

At level three, the highest level of satori from which people return, the point of consciousness becomes a surface or a solid which extends throughout the whole known universe. This used to be called fusion with the Universal Mind or God. In more modern terms you have done a mathematical transformation in which your center of consciousness has ceased to be a traveling point and has become a surface or solid of consciousness. Here you lose the I almost completely although you do retain some memory of this state when you come back. It was in this state that I experienced "myself" as melded and intertwined with hundreds of billions of other beings in a thin sheet of consciousness that is distributed around the galaxy.

KEEN: If a person has this map available can he learn to get into these states of consciousness without using drugs?

LILLY: Yes, drugs may help in the sense that they give some awareness of the existence of different modes and levels of consciousness. Gradually a tolerance is building up in regard to marijuana and LSD, a new kind of permissiveness about all means for the alteration of consciousness. But once you know a space exists you can learn to get back to it. You can program yourself to move into any space you know exists if you use discipline and concentration.

This is the most turned-on country the world has ever seen. The rest of the world is way behind. Our kids are turned on to levels of consciousness and possibilities of travel into mental and spiritual spaces in an unprecedented way.

KEEN: Do you think the consciousness revolution will eventually change the way technology is used?

LILLY: It will improve it immensely.

KEEN: The exploration of inner space is producing a body of new knowledge. Who will disseminate it, and to whom?

LILLY: I see it being transmitted to and within the Establishment. The new exploration of consciousness is a way of life. You will be seeing it on television and in the other media. Already the younger generation is sharing its knowledge of how to alter awareness.

But the people I am most interested in are the successful heads of corporations and bureaucracies. Many of these people already operate at the level of satori 24. They are joyfully locked into their work. But they have never had maps which suggested to them the possibility of achieving more blissful levels of consciousness.

What might happen if they could visualize the possibility of spending the weekend in satori 12, or even of achieving satori three, in which they would realize that their essences are hooked to every other essence in the whole universe?

KEEN: A touch of mystical madness might unite us to non-human forms of consciousness—we might even begin to feel a kinship with other members of our own species.

LILLY: It might turn out that exploring the far-out spaces of human consciousness is the fastest way to social transformation.

Chapter 14

shuffle
brain

Paul Pietsch

Punky was a salamander. Or at least he had the body of a sala-mander. But his cranium housed the brains of a frog. I'd spent an entire season at the fringe of his clear-water world, asking who he was, with the neural juice of a totally different animal racing around inside, turning him on, tuning him in to his environment at a wave band beyond a normal salamander's spectrum. The answers, borne by his actions, flattened my scientific detachment, I confess.

Punky was only one in a long and varied series of brain trans-plants, experimental tests of the holographic theory, a theory about the language of the brain, a scientific treatment of nothing less than memory itself—the watering hole on the great subjective plain where thoughts and dreams, hopes and fears, pride and guilt, love and hate must drink to live, or else dry up, to vanish, like bone dust.

Years before, in Philadelphia, when I was first learning how to do operations like those on Punky, I was an instructor in a gross-anatomy dissecting lab. Class met in the afternoon. Insecure in my grip on what was then a newly acquired subject, I went in early each morning to do a dissection of my own. With class in session, the place roiled with the hurly-burly of people, alive and busy. But in the morning, when I arrived, it was silent, a room of death in the most complete sense of the word. Ugly gray light blared in through frosted windows and, without color, illuminated the rows of rag-swaddled, tarp-wrapped cadavers. It wasn't frightening; it was lonely, the loneliest place I'd ever seen. Its tables were the biers of the world's unwanted, unremembered, unclaimed—as people. And they'd been forgotten long before their corpses were hoisted up and flopped naked on the diener's soapstone prep table. Nameless now, serial-numbered metal-ring tag tied around big toe, dirt still under cracked nail or maybe half-peeled-away red or pink nail polish. Valuable, in death, as things. Valueless before, as people. They were the unloved dead. For to be loved is to be remembered. They were the unhated dead, for the same abstract reasons. The unremembered dead, the truly dead. For memory is our claim to identity, and when it stops, we are no more.

At the end, when we were finished, my department held funeral services for the bodies. I went. But I went with a generalized grief that I carried back whole because my memory found no place to assign any part of it.

Still, in time, I did forget the details. But Punky revived my memories of those mornings back in Philadelphia. That's probably why I gave him a name. For the *Existenz* of Punky and his pals didn't stop with salamanders and frogs. It included my own species.

I will be talking here about the neural hologram, but I really should speak of brain information—a *hologic* principle, not only memory of past experiences. For the theory seeks to explain all the brain's stored programs, whether learned or wired in during embryonic life. It covers the mental yardgoods we unwrap to tailor "go: no-go" in reflexes. It supplies the cash for complex, reasoned associations. It works when the brain issues instructions to tune the A-string on a viola, or to make the baby cry because the milk is sour.

But holographic theory deals with the mode of neural messages, not specific molecules, mechanisms, or cells, as such. Like a multiplication table or counting system, it commits grand polygamy with place and time and circumstance. It treats the *how* rather than the *who*—like gravity acting on the apple, instead of the meat, the freckles, or the worm.

The holographic theory had its crude origins in the 1920s when psychologist Karl Lashley began a lifelong search through the brain for the vaults containing memory. By then, students of behavior had been readied for angry debate by a paradox that had begun to emerge on the surgical tables of the nineteenth century. Clearly, the mental world had its biological base in the brain. Yet war, disease, and the stroke of the scalpel had robbed human brains of substance without necessarily expunging the mind. Lashley carried the problem to the laboratory and pursued it with precision tools, mazes, rats, controls, statistics.

Lashley also brought along the knife. With it, he found he could dull memory in proportion to the amount of cerebrum he cut out. But if he left a rat with any cerebrum at all, the animal could still remember. Not only did he fail to amputate memory, but one area of the cortex would serve it as well as another. He came to two controversial conclusions: intensity of recall depends on the mass of brain, but memory must be divvied up equally. "Mass action" and "equipotentiality" became his theme.

"Equibull!" a neuroanatomist friend of mine once declared. For the knives and battery poles of others had struck and dug into what seemed to be the specific loci of sight, scent, sound. Moreover, no clear and obvious physical precedent existed for equipotentiality. "I'm a scientist," my friend used to say, "not a goddamn Ouija board operator!"

But in 1948 physicist Dennis Gabor, trying to improve the electron microscope, accidentally stumbled over the optical hologram, a discovery that earned him the Nobel Prize in 1971. Lensless, 3-D photography was born. Within twenty years, the same principles had been extended to the brain.

Holograms take getting used to—like the idea that light can be both waves and particles, or that a curve gets you more quickly from star A to star B than Euclid's straight line. It's like getting accustomed to the notion that energy and mass are different ways of saying the same thing, or that time might shrink and expand. For holograms package information in a form disguised from our common sense, invisible behind the nominalistic curtains of our culture. But with patience, and a little open-mindedness, the intuition soon begins to drink up the principles—like relativity after Einstein or the shape of the earth after Columbus.

Familiar modes of information, even as complicated codes, reduce to bit parts, held, stored; according to the *summum bonum* of home economics and gross anatomy: "A place for everything, and everything in its place!" Not so a hologram (*holo* means whole). In it, the entire *shtick* of information, tamped down into a minuscule transcendental code, repeats itself, whole, throughout whatever the system happens to be. Trim a hologram down to a tiny chip and the message still survives, whole, waiting only to be decoded. One piece will work as well as another. But the fewer the parts used in decoding, the less intense the regenerated image. In other words, holograms work in precisely the same way that the memories in Lashley's rats did—mass action and equipotentiality.

. . . A hologram captures not a thingy thing. It captures rules—a harmonic syllogism, a holologic. And it is the stored record of Hegelian skid marks produced when points and counterpoints bang into each other, physical or numerical, concrete or abstract. Mathematics in reverse. Indeed, they take getting used to. But the glory of holograms glows through during decoding back to the original image, when they not only behave like Lashley's rats but reveal feature upon feature of human brain function.

Holographers can construct, say, acoustical holograms and call back the original, not with sound, but with light or waves in some other form. Thus, built into holographic grammar is the automatic mechanism to shift gears, instantly, from one modality to another—how, for example, you can listen to someone and *write* what you *hear* him say as fast as you can work the muscles in your hand.

Such rapid, whole-scene shifts, involving forests of data, would be out of the question with the conventional message that must be translated bit by bit. In a hologram, it's all part and parcel of the principle. And the same thing shows up again in adding and modifying holograms. Holographers can construct multicolored, composite holograms, in steps, by adjusting wavelength, thus mimicking how we might anneal present and past into a totality. Or they can decode several holograms of the same thing into a multicolored original. In the process they can even change colors. When the brain does these things on its munificent scale, we talk in terms of abstract reasoning or imagination. And in this capacity the human brain outshines the largest digital computers. For computers digest bits. But the brain's motifs are informational wholes that can meld and blend without the go-between of a finger-counting bureaucrat.

The flexible rules of holography even allow, automatically, for a subconscious, a bad word in my own particular profession.

But consider an optical hologram. In decoding, it's possible to select a wavelength invisible to the naked eye, yet of sufficient energy to burn a monogram permanently onto the retina of an unwary onlooker. As with the subconscious, you don't have to see its wounds to ache from them.

Holographic theory would also explain the chemical transfer of memory—how information from the brain of one worm, rat, mouse, or hamster might be extracted into a test tube and injected into another animal, there to mediate recall in the absence of the recipient's previous experience. Such reports from a dozen laboratories over the past few years have excited the press and reading public. But in conventional scientific circles, I've heard them called such things as "oozings from the stressed seams of cracked pots." Yet a hologram can write itself into anything, including a molecule. At the very same time, the theory in no way at all restricts the brain's programs to molecules, as such. There's no rule against using, say, molecules, voltages on cells, or groups of neurons to carry the information. The program might even be carried at many different levels simultaneously.

Just who deserves credit as the first to apply holographic principles to the brain I'm going to allow historians of science to fight out. Lashley, of course, saw them at work in his rats and had both the genius and the courage to describe what nature showed. Certain of Pavlov's conclusions look holological. Gabor's powerful mind must have snared the notion the moment he tripped on the optical effect. Years later, in fact, he published a mathematical scheme of reminiscing. Philip Westlake, a brilliant UCLA cyberneticist, has shown that equations of physical holograms match what the brain does with information. Karl Pribram and an army of colleagues at Stanford's medical school have invested a decade and a thousand monkeys, using the theory to work out details of how living brains remember.

Predictably, holographic talk provokes hot controversy. I recall not long ago delivering a lecture on the subject, when out of the audience jumped a neuropharmacologist, trembling with rage, demanding to know: "How can you account for something like Broca's area?" He was referring to a part of the cerebrum known for 100 years to be vulnerable to stroke accompanied by the loss of speech. I cleared my throat to answer. But before I had the chance, a young psychophysicist, sprawled in a front-row seat, whipped his shoulder-length mane around and fired back, "You can't draw beer out of a barrel without a bung!"

It was a perceptive reply. For in holographic theory, functional centers such as Broca's area represent processing stations rather than storage depots. Rage, fear, hunger centers, the visual cortex at the back of the brain, or auditory areas at the sides—these would act not to house specialized information but to pump it in or to call out programs in the form, say, of snarl, smile, utterance, equation, kiss, or thought. And sharp lines of distinction between innate and acquired information fade as far as storage itself is concerned.

Still, the theory does not completely rule out uneven distribution of memory, particularly in the complex brains of higher animals. Indeed, it is not hard to make a case for different storage within the two hemispheres of the human cerebrum. Michael Gazzaniga recently published an intriguing book on what has been known for almost twenty years as "split-brain" research. Begun in the early 1950s by Meyers and Sperry at Cal Tech, the technique involves cutting the corpus callosum, a broad thick strap of nerve fibers between the hemispheres. Success in the lab with cats and monkeys prompted neurosurgeons to split the corpus callosum in the human brain. They did so to alleviate violent, prolonged, drug-resistant grand mal epileptic seizures, and they had remarkable success, medically. But the patients emerged from surgery with two permanently disconnected personalities. With more such operations, the left cerebral hemisphere emerged as the dominant, verbal, arithmetic side, while the right brain held recollections of form and texture. The tendencies appear to hold whether patients were left- or right-handed. Early in 1971, music was found among the repertoire of the right hemisphere. Yet the outcome of split-brain surgery has never been absolute, nor the individual patient's subsequent behavior totally predictable. Both hemispheres can generate music in some people, and the right may have a vocabulary. In addition, a totally illiterate right hemisphere can learn to read and write in less than six months—as though it had a tremendous head start. On top of this, Gazzaniga's observations convince him that the consignment of memories to one side of the brain emerges with maturity. Children seem to employ both hemispheres. Thus it would seem that the brain can reshape its contents and make decisions about what will go where. But it is also quite possible that split-brain research identifies not unequal storage but unequal access. Like the reflected image of a written message, meaning would stay the same but translation would entail different steps. The cerebral hemispheres, after all, do mirror rather than carbon-copy each other.

At any rate, the brains of human beings and our close relatives seem to be many brains, orchestrated by virtue of connections like the corpus callosum. Moreover, our multisystem cranial contents seem to be in flux, physiologically. Different lights can flash off and on, moment to moment. Some of the switches lie under our direct control; others are no more within our deliberate, intellectual reach than the impulses driving a hungry shark or an amorous jackrabbit.

Holographic theory does not deny conclusions of split-brain research. But it insists that, whatever the system used for storage, the information shall be layered in whole and repeated throughout. It denies that memory depends on minced-up and isolated bits filed in specific pigeonholes. Just what happens to be going on inside a brain when it's loading up with a particular hologram may determine which areas may and may not act as targets—or how vivid the reconstructed scene becomes during some later translation into conscious form.

THEORIES AND EXPERIMENTS

. . . My purpose in working with Punky and his pals was to make or break my faith in the holographic theory of neural storage. And I was a skeptic, at the outset.

When I began this work the only prima facie experimental evidence to link the general theory involving holographic principles to brains had come from ablation studies—subtracting from brain substance. Subtraction is an incomplete test. To see the incompleteness is to see how the salamanders relate to the theory. Thus, let's spend a little time doing a few imaginary experiments.

Imagine several hundred Xerox copies of this unholographic page, but reproduced on transparent plastic sheets. Now stack the sheets so that each letter, word, and line forms a perfect overlay with its replicates below. Now subtract a sheet—two, three, or any number, for that matter—only keeping the stack straight. What happens? Loss or unevenness in density, perhaps. But as long as we keep the *equivalence* of one page, we preserve the message. The reasons are obvious. First, we're working with a system containing a redundant message. Secondly, when we eliminated some parts, we merely allowed what was beneath to shine through. But we certainly don't have a holographic system. This is how I viewed the results of ablation studies.

Let's try another series of experiments with the transparencies. Let's throw the pile up in the air, arrange some of the sheets in a new order, cut some of the sheets into pieces and reglue the pieces randomly—reshuffle, in other words. Now we would distort the message and know it very quickly. Why? *Meaning* in a conventional message (or pattern) depends on relationships *among* parts and subparts—sets and subsets. When we scrambled relationships, when we messed up the system's anatomy, we wrenched the carriers of meaning. We might also have done this by adding a transparency with a different message. But when we merely took away parts from our redundant system, we created empty sets and voided rather than distorted relationships.

But suppose the linotype operator had set a hologram? Then our reshuffling experiments would have produced far different results. We would not have introduced changes in the meaning of the message. For in a hologram meaning lies *within*—not among—any sets we might produce by simple physical means. And in reshuffling we would be shifting whole messages around, exchanging their positions without really getting at components. Trying to dissect out a hologram's subunits is like trying to slice a point, or stretch that infinitesimally small domain by an amount no larger than itself. No, a knife won't reach inside the heart of a hologram. Of course, in practice we might trim a system to such small proportions that the image upon decoding would be too dim to register. Or in a physical experiment we could destroy or distort the medium and make it technically impossible to decode. That's why we opted for imagination—to bypass engineering details.

But look at the implications of our imaginary experiments. Look at the predictions. If we really want to test holography against redundancy, we ought to shuffle the brain. If it houses conventional messages, we would find out very quickly. But if programs exist in the brain according to holographic principles, scramble though we may, we won't distort their meanings. And that is where salamanders come in.

BRAIN TRANSPLANT

A peaceful, quiet world, the salamander's—unless you happen to be a dainty little daphnia or a cockeyed mosquito larva whiplashing to the surface for a gulp of air. Or even worse, the crimson thread of a tubifex worm. For it is the destiny of the salamander to detect, pursue, and devour all moving morsels of meat small enough to fit inside his mouth. He eats only what moves. And he adjusts his attack to fit the motion of his fated quarry. When he sees the tubifex worm, or picks it up on sonar with his lateral line organs, he lets you know with a turn of his head. Position fixed, half-swimming, half-walking, he glides slowly, deliberately, along the bottom of his dish, careful not to create turbulence that, in the wilds, would send the worm burrowing deep into the safety of the mud. Reaching his victim, he coasts around it, moving his head back and forth, up and down, to catch swelling and shrinking shadows and vibrations and permit his tiny brain to compute the tensor calculus of the worm's ever-changing size.

The size of a four-year-old's little finger, salamanders sustain injury and recuperate like few other creatures on earth. Consider, for example, what I call the Rip Van Winkle paradigm. Remove a salamander's brain. The behaviorally inert body continues to live, indefinitely. Transplant the brain to the animal's broad, jelly-filled tail fin for storage. After a month or two, slide the brain out of the fin and return it to the empty cranium. In a couple of weeks, after the replant takes, the animal behaves as if the operation had never occurred. He's awake again, a free-living, prowling organism, like his normal brothers and sisters.

That same tail fin will accommodate hunks of brain pooled ad hoc from several different salamanders. The pieces quickly send out thousands of microscopic nerve fibers that weave a confluent network. Does such a mass of brain tissue work? Communicate impulses? Splice a length of spinal cord on each end of the mass as a conduit to the skin. Then, on one side, graft an eye, pressing the cut optic nerve against the piece of spinal cord. On the other side transplant a leg, making sure that it touches the conduit. Wait a couple of weeks to allow the optic nerve to invade the spinal cord on the one side and the cord on the other to sprout fibers into the leg to reinnervate its muscles. Now aim a spotlight at the tail and focus on the grafted eye. If you can hit the light switch at the correct tempo, you can make the transplanted leg stomp a tarantella.

Yet if my experiments were to be a fair test of the holographic theory, I'd have to insure two things. First, the experimental salamander would have to be capable of sensing a tubifex worm. Secondly, he'd have to be able to command his body and jaw muscles into action. I was sure this could be done with salamanders by preserving the medulla, the transitional region between spinal cord and the rest of the brain. In the medulla lie input stations for touch from the head, the salamander's efficient sonar system, and the sense of balance from a carpenter's level like internal ear. Also, impulses that bring jaw muscles snapping to life are issued directly from the medulla. It does for head muscles what the spinal cord does for, say, the biceps or muscles in the thigh. And in salamanders the medulla serves as a relay station for information to and from spinal cord and brain. Higher animals have such stations too. But evolution added long tracts that function like neural expressways.

There are actually five main parts of the brain common to all vertebrates, including man. The cerebral hemispheres that predominate within our own heads are small lobes on the tip end of a salamander's brain. But during embryonic life our own cerebral hemispheres pass through a salamander stage.

The next region back, known as the diencephalon, is where the optic nerves enter the brain. Distorting this region would and did create blindness in certain experiments. A so-called messencephalon or mid-brain connects diencephalon to medulla. These were the parts I would shuffle.

Amputating brain in front of the medulla turned off the salamander's conscious behavior and, of course, feeding along with it. But, if I stayed out in front of the medulla, I'd be leaving sufficient input and output intact for whatever programs surgery might deliver up.

This is not surgery in the nurse-mask-sutures-and-blood sense. It goes on under a stereoscopic microscope. Very little bleeding. No stitches. Just press the sticky, cut tissues together and permit armies of mobilized cells to swarm over and obscure the injured boundary line. There is only room in the field of operation for a single pair of human hands. The animals sleep peacefully in anesthetic dissolved in the water. Trussed lightly against cream-colored marble clay, magnified, they look like the prehistoric giants of their ancestry. A strong heart thrusts battalions of red blood corpuscles through a vascular maze of transparent tissues. No bones to saw. Under fluid your instruments coax like a sable-hair brush.

In more than 700 operations, I rotated, reversed, added, subtracted, and scrambled brain parts. I shuffled. I reshuffled. I sliced, lengthened, deviated, shortened, apposed, transposed, juxtaposed, and flipped. I spliced front to back with lengths of spinal cord, of medulla, with other pieces of brain turned inside out. But nothing short of dispatching the brain to the slop bucket—nothing expunged feeding!

Some operations created permanent blindness, forcing animals to rely on their sonar systems to tell them what was going on outside. But the optic nerves of salamanders can regenerate. Still, for normal vision to return, regenerating optic nerves need a suitable target, as Roger Sperry showed many years ago. I was able to arrange for this, surgically. And when I did, eyesight recovered completely in about two weeks—even when the brains came from a totally different species of salamander and contained extra parts. As far as feeding was concerned, nature continued to smile on holography. Not one single thing about the behavior of this group of animals suggested the drastic surgery they had undergone.

The experiments had subjected the holographic theory to a severe test. As the theory predicted, scrambling the brain's anatomy did not scramble its programs. Meaning was contained within the parts, not spread out among their relationships. If I wanted to change behavior, I had to supply not a new anatomy but new information.

Suppose, though, that parts of a salamander brain in front of the medulla really have no direct relationship to what a salamander does with a worm? Suppose feeding stations exist in the medulla or spinal cord (or left leg), awaiting only consciousness to ignite them? If this were true, the attack response on worms—the principal criterion in the study—would be irrelevant, and shuffle brain experiments would say very little about the holographic theory. A purist might have taken care of this issue at the outset.

"New experiments required," I scribbled in my notes. "Must have following features. Host: salamander minus brain anterior to medulla. Donor: try a vegetarian, maybe young Rana pipiens tadpole. But, first, make damn sure donor brain won't actively shut off salamander's attack on worms."

My working hunch was that the very young leopard frog tadpole would make a near-perfect donor. His taste for flies comes much later on in development. While he's little, he'll mimp-mouth algae from the flanks of a tubifex and harm nothing but a little vermigrade pride. Then, too, from experiments I'd carried out years before, I knew frog tissues wouldn't manifestly offend salamander rejection mechanisms, not to the extent that they would be destroyed. Thus, if grafted brains didn't perish in transit across the operating dish, they would become permanent fixtures in their new heads.

Whether a tadpole brain would or would not actively shut off worm-recognition programs in salamanders I had to settle experimentally before calling Punky into the game. Here, I transplanted tadpole brain parts but left varying amounts of host salamander brain in place. These animals ate normally, thus showing that tadpole brain, per se, would not overrule existing attack programs. As I had guessed, it was like adding a zero to a string of integers as far as feeding was concerned.

Now the scene was ready for Punky, the first of his kind through the run. He would surrender his own cranial contents in front of the medulla to the entire brain of a frog. If his new brain restored consciousness but gave him a tadpole's attitude about worms, he'd vindicate the shuffle brain experiments.

For controls, I carried out identical operations but used other salamanders as donors. Also, to assure myself that frog tissue itself would not affect appetite, I inserted diced tadpole in the fins and body cavities of still other salamanders. This procedure had no effect on feeding. Moreover, I had a hunch that Punky would remain blind. So I removed eyes from other salamanders to get fresh data on feeding via sonar.

Punky awoke on the seventeenth day. Very quickly, he became one of the liveliest, most curious-acting animals in the lab. He did remain blind but his sonar more than compensated. A fresh worm dropped into his bowl soon brought him over. He'd nose around the worm for several minutes. He lacked the tadpole's sucker mouth. And I couldn't decide whether he wanted algae, or what. But he spent a lot of time with the worms. In the beginning, he had me watching him, wondering in a pool of clammy sweat if he'd uncork and devour the holographic theory in a single chomp. Yet, during three months, with a fresh worm in his bowl at all times, in more than 1,800 direct encounters, Punky never made so much as a single angry pass at a tubifex. Nor did any of his kind in the months that followed. The herbivorous brain had changed the worms' role in the paradigm. They were to play with now, not to ravage.

I kept Punky's group nourished by force-feeding them fresh fillets of salamander once a week. This meant the same thing had to be done with each and every control animal too. While the extra food did not blunt control appetites, the added work left me looking groggily toward pickling time when I could preserve the specimens on microscopic slides.

I routinely examine microscopic slides as a final ritual. But Punky's slides weren't routine. And on the very first section I brought into sharp focus, the truth formed a fully closed circle in the barrel of my microscope. His tadpole brain, indeed, had survived. It stood still in terms of development, but it was a nice, healthy organ. And from its hind end emerged a neural cable. The cable penetrated Punky's medulla, there to plunge new holographic ideas into his salamander readout, and into the deepest core of my own beliefs.

Chapter 15

tomorrow we will

communicate

to our jobs

Peter C. Goldmark

I would like you to join me in exploring how we could make use of communications technology on a much broader scale to ensure that in the year 2000 the United States will be a wonderful place in which to live and to work, whether one chooses the city or prefers the country.

Before we discuss solutions, let us look at the problem:

One of the disturbing effects of the rapidly increasing population is that the majority of people in most western countries have been compelled to live under conditions of extreme density, within the confines of cities and their suburbs. Today, nine-tenths of the United States population lives on less than 10 percent of the land.

If this trend continues, 200 million of the 300 million Americans anticipated for the year 2000 will be crowded into twelve urban centers on less than 10 percent of our total land area. More than half of the population, or 150 million people, will be in the three largest urban concentrations, namely: Boston-Washington, Chicago-Pittsburgh, San Francisco-San Diego.

Man is physiologically and psychologically unprepared for the stresses and strains which result from such living conditions. Available statistics show that it is in the high-density living areas

"Tomorrow We Will Communicate to Our Jobs," by Peter C. Goldmark. From *The Futurist*, April 1972 (vol. 6, no. 2). Published by the World Future Society, Bethesda Branch, Washington, D.C. Reprinted by permission of the publisher.

that the problems of crime, pollution, poverty, traffic, education, etc., are the greatest.

Experience has shown that the problems are manageable in smaller towns and will remain so, if limits and standards are carefully planned for the development of these towns.

Today, in addition to our urban problems, we also have a rural problem. There exists a large migration of people from rural areas towards urban centers. The depopulation of rural areas has depressed them economically, and left many of them unable to provide the services that their residents need.

We now have roughly outlined the problem. Let us see what might be a solution. The more than 50 million Americans expected to be added to our population by the year 2000 should be able to live and work in either an improved urban or a new rural environment. To make this possible, a new rural society must be created. In this task, communications technology plays a key role.

In 1968, the President's Advisory Group on Telecommunications requested the National Academy of Engineering (NAE) to establish a committee on telecommunications. As an outgrowth of the President's request, the NAE created a panel for applying communications technology to alleviate urban problems and to make possible new living patterns based on fuller use of the nation's land resources. The NAE panel later joined with the Connecticut Research Commission (CRC) to form the NAE-CRC Joint Committee on "Cities of the Future," which I chair. The NAE panel is supported by a joint group consisting of the Departments of Housing and Urban Development, Justice, Commerce, Transportation, Health Education and Welfare, and also the U.S. Postal Service, and the Federal Communications Commission. *It is our belief that all necessary inventions have already been made and broadband communications systems now can be imaginatively applied to the needs of business, government, education, health care, and cultural pursuits to stimulate the development of the new rural society. The task is gigantic: It will present an urgent challenge to our youth, and all of us must direct at least part of our efforts to it. I believe the magnitude of this task will make going to the moon seem like a ferryboat ride.*

The approach to the new rural society does not mean the deurbanization of America. In our opinion, the main objective is to provide options for the additional millions of people, options which today do not exist. Conceivably half of the next 100 million Americans may prefer to live in an urban environment, whereas 50 million people already in the cities may wish to be part of the new rural society. This in itself may relieve the pressure on the cities, making it feasible to deal with their most urgent problems and to start them on a new life cycle.

We must recognize that to change the entire nation's living pattern requires more than communications technology alone. Before nationwide planning is undertaken, an exploratory program on a small scale is proposed in the attractive rural northeastern section of Connecticut where the population density is low and the need for planned economic development is high. This project is being funded by the U.S. Department of Housing and Urban Development in cooperation with Fairfield University. The first study phase is expected to begin shortly in Connecticut's Windham County Region, a slightly undeveloped area of approximately 650 square miles and involving ten townships. The study will be conducted jointly by Fairfield University and Goldmark Communications Corporation.

FOUR-PART PROGRAM TO HALT MIGRATION TO CITIES

Our "Cities of the Future" committee proposes a four-part experimental program designed to halt the migration of people from rural areas to the cities and to reverse the continuing trend of urban deterioration:

1. Study the office procedures and practices that usually result in meetings, memos, letters, presentations, etc., in business, industry and government. How can these procedures be transposed into broadband and other communications media? The results of the study should indicate how components of business or government could function effectively in rural communities.

2. Join with a number of towns in a given region in exploring how to establish standards and limits which will ensure the optimum rate and pattern of growth for the highest quality of life. The effort should be coordinated with relevant State agencies to assure that the development program is in the best overall interests of

the State, and should establish the need for utilities, transportation, and other resources in line with the growth goals.

3. Experiment with a variety of communications equipment that could provide the services necessary for the business, government, and other aspects of life of the developing community.

4. Create an intergovernmental body of federal and state officials to initiate a coordinated, national effort based on the experiences gained by the study project.

NEW RURAL SOCIETY WILL EMERGE

We would like to give all Americans an opportunity to work and live in small but attractive rural communities. The persons who choose to settle in these communities will become the new rural society.

The society that we envision does not now exist because, in general, people do not want to move into a rural area, no matter how attractive, unless it offers jobs, adequate educational and health services, opportunities for cultural pursuits, entertainment, social contacts, and so on.

The British have long explored a solution to their own high-density population problems, and they are way ahead of us in creating new towns and enlarging old ones. In 1944, the Abercrombie Plan for Greater London provided for the establishment of a whole series of new towns around London, beyond the so called Green Belt.

The purpose of the plan was to relieve the concentration in Inner-London; to provide a better working and living environment; and to reduce the length of commuting trips. While thirty-one new towns were built and succeeded in attracting business and industry, office employment in London continues to expand. Clearly, the rate of generating new towns is not fast enough.

The British government concluded that the largest deterrent to decentralizing is likely to be the reduction in operating efficiency due to the stretching of communication links.

Another British study was made by a group called Joint Unit for Planning Research, which has engaged in one of the most thorough and controlled experiments in communications between widely separated operations. The Study concluded that:

1. The ordinary telephone is highly effective for one-to-one communications, particularly where familiarity between participants is high, conflict is low, and subject matter is well defined.

2. The greatest value of a wideband network suitable for television or picture-phone will lie in its ability to handle a wide range of auxiliary services such as graphics display, rapid facsimile, computer and data access, conferencing, etc.

3. There will be large-scale decentralization of employment from large metropolitan centers as the various person-to-person telecommunications systems improve.

4. The effect on the volume of business travel is likely to be negligible.

5. Most importantly, the chief effect of such telecommunication developments will be to increase the choices: The employee will be able to select the environment he wants to live in, and a company or government agency will have a wider choice of areas in which to locate.

It may be interesting to observe that in pursuit of their ruralization plans the British are currently designing broad band services on four fronts: (1) a national data network, (2) conference television, (3) dedicated cable educational television for the London area, and (4) household wired television.

FIVE NETWORKS FOR THE NEW RURAL COMMUNITY

Let us examine the services that communications technology can provide to a new rural community.

New communication networks could be divided into internal and external systems. The internal system, which is strictly within the bounds of towns, will consist of five basic networks:

Network One:

The primary network exists now only in the form of the telephone. It would be expanded into a full two-way random-access network able to accommodate voice, data, and two-way video-phone. This would be the most basic urban "nerve system" which will be as vital as streets, water, or power. *The most basic purpose of this system would be to put everyone in contact with everyone else within the city, no matter how dark the streets are, how heavy the traffic.* Since it will be linked up with computers, the same network will provide random access between man and machine, or between machines. *The network can be looked upon as providing a pipe into every home, office or library through which one can not only converse, but also transmit and receive written materials, pictures, data, etc.* Its most important contribution is to connect every terminal (telephone, videophone, teletype writer, etc.) with any other.

Network Two:

A second network would be in the form of AM-FM radio and television broadcasting, the extent depending on the channels available for the particular community. This could consist of one or more local stations preferably with network affiliations and educational television broadcasting.

Network Three:

The third internal network would be in the form of broadband cables carrying a multitude of television channels into individual homes. This network would include narrowband call-back for purposes of polling or making requests. Such two-way cable television systems are now already being tested. The cable network could also carry, if desired, off-the-air programs, originating either from local broadcast stations or from satellites. This cable network should be so designed that it has sub-centers in the local neighborhood which, in terms of program material, could cater to its own local audience. *As part of this network, general informational services would be made available to individual homes. One important example would be the ability to dial up important municipal events, such as meetings of the various town boards, i.e., Education, Finance, Zoning, Board of Representatives, etc. Through the network's two-way polling ability, public opinion on any issue under discussion could be almost instantly registered. Through a system of "frame freezing," vast amounts of information concerning travel, weather, pollution, shopping, traffic, various municipal and other public services, lists of cultural and entertainment events, etc., could be selected and seen on the home television screen.*

Network Four:

The fourth information network superimposed on the town would be another broadband cable system, carrying approximately forty two-way television channels which would interconnect the major public institutions of the city: city hall, hospitals and nursing homes, schools and colleges, libraries, police and fire stations, bus and railroad stations, airports, and all other town services. This network would provide informational services among the vital institutions and key officials of town, ensuring their smooth operation.

Network Five:

Superimposed on the preceding four networks would be a town emergency service. This would include the "911" police and fire emergency system augmented by automatic identification of a caller's location and by a system to identify the location of vehicles operated by police, fire, sanitation, ambulance, utilities, and other large fleet operations.

In addition to the five networks making up the internal communication systems, the city of the future will have external systems, consisting of the following:

1. Incoming broadband cable or microwave circuits which connect the town's businesses, industry and government offices with their operations in other cities or countries. These are essentially dedicated point-to-point links.

2. Long-distance broadband circuits interconnecting the town's switched telephone and video-phone services with the corresponding switched services in other cities.

3. Common carrier broadband and narrow band services such as U.S. Postal Service, Western Union, and others for transmission of messages, printed material, data, etc., between towns and to other countries.

4. Incoming circuits for educational, cultural and recreational pursuits. These might include:
   a. Radio and television broadcast circuits both for private networks and public broadcasting.

b. Two-way broadband educational television circuits interconnecting a small local campus with the region's central university.

c. Broadband cable circuit as part of a national high-definition closed circuit television network bringing live Broadway, opera, concert and sports productions to theaters especially geared for such performances. The system would employ high resolution color television of at least 1,000 lines with cameras and projectors especially designed for live pick-up and large screen projection. The most suitable national distribution method for such signals may be through a synchronous satellite broadcasting several of these high-definition TV signals and received by local high-gain fixed antennas.

All these communication systems, properly integrated on a national basis, will go a long way toward realizing the New Rural Society.

I apologize that in this limited space we could only sample certain aspects of this very ambitious but essential plan. A beginning has been made, but for the ideas to become reality, scientists and engineers of this and the next generation must help. Very simply, this is an opportunity for science and technology to make one of its greatest contributions to man and his environment.